Romans
The Heart Set Free

Other books by Gordon Ferguson

Discipling: God's Plan to Train and Transform His People

Love One Another

Mine Eyes Have Seen the Glory

Revolution: The World-changing Church in the Book of Acts

Prepared to Answer

The Power of Gratitude

The Power of Spiritual Thinking

The Power of Discipling

The Victory of Surrender

Romans
The Heart Set Free

GORDON FERGUSON

DPI
DISCIPLESHIP
PUBLICATIONS
INTERNATIONAL

Romans

© 2001 by Discipleship Publications International
2 Sterling Road, Billerica, Mass. 01862-2595

Printed in the United States of America
ISBN: 1-57782-168-8

Cover Design: Christine Nolan & Tony Bonazzi
Interior Design: Corey Fisher

Dedication

Romans has been my favorite *book* of the Bible for many years. I would not want to think of what my life might have been like without this precious book. It has challenged me, comforted me, led me and motivated me like no other portion of Scripture.

In a similar way, my favorite *human being* for many years has been—and always will be—my wife, Theresa. I shudder to think what I would have been like had I not married her nearly thirty-seven years ago. She has challenged me, comforted me, often led me by example and motivated me like no one else. In a very real sense, she has shown me the principles of Romans in her life, and in her love for me, because she has been a consistent imitator of Jesus for a long time.

Theresa is to me grace embodied on a daily basis. She has endured patiently through my earliest years as a worldly pagan and then through many subsequent years as a religious Pharisee. In all of these challenges, she continued to love me *unconditionally*. She was gentle in expressing her desires to have a more spiritual husband and father for her children. She almost never nagged, in spite of the frustrations with which she consistently lived. I rarely felt a heavy sense of disappointment or disapproval from her, although I was aware of the areas in my life that she wanted me to change. She demonstrated that rare but godly quality of calling me higher without being down on me.

It would take many pages of writing to even come close to expressing what she means to me as my wife, my constant companion, my best friend, my romantic lover par excellence, and my coworker for the Lord. When God ushers me into my eternal home, it will be because he chose to demonstrate his grace to me, not only in his Son and in his word, but also through the woman he gave to me.

Theresa, thank you so much for being that *unique* helper perfectly suited to make me a whole person before God and men. I love you with all my heart in a way that will never end, for you are my sister in Christ, as well as my dearly beloved wife.

Contents

Righteousness Results in Real Relationships

Preface

My Own Pilgrimage in Search of Grace

In talking about living in a state of grace and forgiveness, I often say that we do not play "hopscotch," jumping out of grace when we sin and back into grace when we repent. Interestingly, my understanding of the subject in the past was definitely of the "hopscotch" variety. I began my religious training in what I often call a "mainline Church of Christ." In this group, being sure of one's personal salvation was not part of the package. In that setting, my understanding of grace was virtually nil.

As a young married couple, Theresa and I were fortunate to find a group within this movement that was led by a minister who had a far better grasp of grace than anyone I had ever known. Looking back at those several years, I still am amazed at how much my heart was impacted by the friendship and teaching of a man named Richard Hostetler.[1] Thanks to his influence, things that are often viewed as duties by Christians were for me then seen as great privileges. He demonstrated unconditional acceptance far beyond anything I had experienced, and his teaching was filled with Scripture and inspiration. He knew how to free the heart rather than just engage the head or convict the conscience, although he did the latter two in the process.

Thinking back to the content of his sermons, I remember three major emphases: the grace of God, evangelism and total commitment. But perhaps more important to me was his ability to personally demonstrate grace in his relationship with me. He knew that when I first began attending the congregation where he preached, I was still pretty worldly in both attitudes and actions. Yet he was very patient and noncondemning, evidently realizing that I was going to be difficult to extricate from the world. He never tried to force me to move faster than my heart was changing. And it was changing—to my own amazement. For whatever reason, he reached out to me and built a friendship, although

9

there were many other young married men that would surely have appeared better prospects than I for leadership development. His obvious love for me, the Bible and the God of the Bible put me in touch with grace in a way that turned my world upside down.

Theresa and I simply began to fall in love with God, his Son, the church and spiritual things in general. We began doing so well that I was encouraged by many people to think about becoming a minister. After a few years under Richard's tutelage, I felt the call to formally train for the ministry. (In our church bulletin, he quipped that I had been "called to preach" by waking up at midnight craving chicken—commonly referred to back then as the "gospel bird," the normal table fare at Sunday dinners with the preacher!) The school I then attended was called a "preacher training school," designed to train those who were past college age and desirous of changing careers.

For a number of months, I thought I had died and gone to heaven. Studying the Bible all day (and most of the night) was a welcome obsession. I could not get enough of it! I loved the tests, the memory work, the fellowship of others with like mind, and the early experiences of trying to teach and preach what I was learning. However, as good as it all seemed to be, a rather insidious mind-set began to attach itself to my soul—that of a legalism not dissimilar to what I had experienced in that little church I spoke of earlier.

Thus, that particular school represented for me the best of times and the worst of times. I learned a tremendous amount about the Bible in a brief two-year period. However, the focus of the school was more than conservative: it was legalistically rigid. The grace focus with which I entered gradually gave way to a prideful legalism, as Paul said could happen in 1 Corinthians 8:1: "Knowledge puffs up, but love builds up." My mind became filled with facts, but my heart was filled with doubts regarding the grace of God.

After graduation, I began my first official preaching job as an assistant of sorts under an older preacher. Soon his theology became apparent—he was all grace and no law in his emphases. To say that we clashed a bit is to put it mildly. I could not understand where he was coming from, nor could I understand where those who were influenced by him ended up doctrinally. I remember distinctly when one of the elders of that church taught a midweek class and made this statement: "I have been preaching for many years and serving as an elder for a number of years, but I have just now come to understand what grace is all about. If we are in Christ, we don't have any rules or regulations." He and the rest of that preacher's little "grace group" were at one end of the spectrum (cheap grace), and I was at the other (too legalistic).

The great thing about that unsettling experience is that it forced me to examine my Biblical views rather intensely, which led me to see that I too had some misconceptions. A few years later, when I began working on a graduate degree in New Testament studies, most of my research was in the areas of law and grace. Many of those whom I heard teaching on the subject claimed that the Old Testament was strictly a legal system demanding perfection, with damnation the natural consequence of imperfection. If that were true, then no one could have been saved during the Mosaic Law period. The end result of my studies convinced me that there were some people saved under the OT law, and they must have been saved by grace through faith, just as those under the NT covenant are.[2] Further, I learned most of what I know about Romans and Galatians during those days.

I have always been most grateful for the testing of my faith at the hands of someone I disagreed with, both then and now, for it led me into a richer understanding of grace than I likely would have gained otherwise.

In the intervening years since that time, I believe that I have come to see deeper into the truths of Romans and am happy to be able to pass this understanding on to you, the reader. However, I will confess that I still at times find it difficult to accept these truths deeply in my emotions. I have the accused type of conscience and have more difficulty forgiving myself than God has forgiving me. The solution for me at those times is to once again retrace my steps through Romans and related passages. When I do that, my heart settles again into the peace of God that surpasses understanding (Philippians 4:7).

Only when we come to understand the God described in Romans will our hearts truly be set free. To that end I write and to that end I pray—for you and for me. Let's dig deeply into the truth that will set our hearts and consciences free. May the Maker and Lover of our souls help us to see him clearly and to understand how he sees us!

Notes

1. See the introduction to my book *Discipling: God's Plan to Train and Transform His People* (Billerica, Mass.: Discipleship Publications International, 1997), 12-16, for another account of how Richard won my heart over to him and to Jesus.

2. For a synopsis of some of these studies, see my paper entitled "The Relationship of Grace, Law and Love" in *The Leader's Resource Handbook* (Billerica, Mass.: Discipleship Publications International, 1997), 148-155.

I

Righteousness Begins with
Conviction by the Spirit

Introduction

Why Did Paul Write Romans?

The book of Romans, properly understood, is perhaps the most motivational book in the New Testament because of its focus on the love of God—the best motivation possible. Other motivations may turn us in the direction of God, but only understanding his grace and his all-encompassing love for us will keep us with him for a lifetime. The "fear of the Lord is the beginning of knowledge" (Proverbs 1:7), but love must be the end of it. However, we cannot really appreciate his love until we understand the depth of our sin problem. Romans goes to great lengths to establish both subjects as it expands on Paul's statement in Romans 11:22: "Consider therefore the kindness and sternness of God." Before proceeding to Romans 1, it is first absolutely essential that we understand the background issues that led to the writing of Romans.

Background Issues in Romans

While the historical situation in Rome is not as important to us as the theological situation, it is nevertheless good to understand that Paul was sending this letter to the church in the empire's greatest city. This was a major church that Paul had not started. He had hopes of making his first visit there soon, and the letter may have served to introduce the disciples in Rome to the most crucial aspects of Paul's teaching. It is likely that he wrote this about 58 AD, probably while staying the winter in Corinth. It also seems likely that Phoebe, who is referred to Romans 16:1-2, had been given the letter to take with her to Rome. The more important issues to understand had to do with the way people were thinking about being made right with God.

The Conflict Between Jews and Gentiles

Many Jewish Christians thought that the Gentile Christians were second-class citizens unless they basically accepted the

Judaic mind-set. Since the Jews were the first group in the church and had history with God, they initially exerted much influence on the thinking of the Gentiles. Conflicts arose over circumcision, foods, special days and other aspects of Judaism. Jewish misconceptions about the basis of salvation lay at the root of much of their self-righteousness. As a whole, they confused physical election as a nation with spiritual election as individuals. But being in the "chosen race" did not guarantee them salvation, nor does being on a church membership roll guarantee such in our day. The issue is not as much what our group is doing as it is what kind of faith we as individuals have.

The Jews' greatest misconception was that they were good enough to be saved. In Luke 18:9-14, we find a rare case of Jesus explaining the interpretation of the parable before even giving it. A cursory reading of the passage will provide a clear picture of the Pharisaic attitude of "God is lucky to have me on his side." As disciples, we can share a similarly dangerous attitude in that we can begin "with the Spirit" at baptism (trusting grace) but afterward be guilty of "trying to attain [our] goal by human effort" (trusting works—Galatians 3:3).

Those early Jews were not the only ones with misconceptions about the Old Testament, for present misconceptions about it abound today in religious circles. The Old Testament was not intended to be merely a legal system in God's plan. This mistaken assertion is based on misinterpretations of Romans and Galatians. These two books were written to show the fallacy of holding to a "works" mentality and to show how the law was being wrongly viewed and misused in the first century. Unless we understand these basic issues, we cannot understand Romans and Galatians.

The Jews had always tended to trust in externals rather than internals (are we really any different?). Such misplaced trust leads rapidly to legalism. The book of Deuteronomy was given to the second generation of the Jews to emphasize heart motivation, for the first generation had already missed the key issue of faith trusting in grace. During their captivity period (with their temple destroyed and the people away from their homeland), the Jews' legalism worsened due to the fact that every aspect of their religion was gone except for the law. Thus, they began to rely on it more than ever, as Jesus' words indicate: "You diligently study the Scriptures because you think that by them you possess eternal life" (John 5:39). Regardless of the extent of their misconceptions, we must keep in mind that people living under the Old Testament were to be saved in the same basic way as those living in any age—*by grace through faith*!

The Doctrinal Heart of Romans

Salvation by grace through faith is not the means to salvation solely in the Christian era—it has always been the only means to salvation, including during the OT period. Grace is God's part of the salvation equation, which ultimately finds its expression in the cross of Christ. Hebrews 9:15 says specifically that the death of Jesus was for the forgiveness of sins committed under the first covenant, and Romans 3:25 goes back further, to the beginning of the human race. Faithful people who lived before the cross were saved by the cross, because it was a reality in the mind of God before the crucifixion ever occurred. Revelation 13:8 refers to Jesus as the "Lamb that was slain from the creation of the world," while 2 Peter 3:8 informs us that time means nothing to God ("a day is like a thousand years, and a thousand years are like a day"). Therefore, he could treat a person in the Old Testament as forgiven before (from man's viewpoint) the real basis of forgiveness had actually occurred. As time-bound humans, we may have difficulty understanding this concept, but rest assured that God has no problem with it at all!

Faith is man's part of the salvation process, but "faith" is a many-faceted word. Perhaps Hebrews 11:6 provides us with the best definition of a saving faith, for it is both comprehensive yet concise:

> *And without faith it is impossible to please God, because anyone who comes to him must believe that he exists and that he rewards those who earnestly seek him.*

This passage identifies three aspects of the kind of faith that pleases God: belief, trust and obedience. God's communication in the Bible comes to us in the form of facts, promises and commands. Not surprisingly, faith responds to each of the types of communication. We *believe* the *facts* in the Bible; we *trust* the *promises* in the Bible; and we *obey* the *commands* in the Bible. Therefore, faith that pleases God is having the appropriate response to his word. We cannot obey a fact, nor can we simply believe a command. We must match our response to the form of teaching found, thereby taking God at his word.

Keep in mind that God's part (grace) is the true foundation or basis of forgiveness, while man's part (faith) is only a condition of accepting this mercy. The sacrifice of Christ actually *merits* forgiveness, and the latter simply *accepts* it. Grace is God giving us what we need rather than what we deserve, and our understanding of this process keeps us God-reliant rather than self-reliant. Therefore, faith must focus on trusting the firm ground of forgiveness—grace, expressed most fully in the cross—not our response to the graceful conditions of God. And this principle is true whether the designated condition was an animal sacrifice in the Old Testament or is a response specified in the New Testament. Neither action earns salvation but only accepts it with a heart of trust in God, full of gratitude. (See Psalm 51:16-19.)

For example baptism is the way we initially accept salvation, not the basis or meriting factor of it. Ideally, we all felt totally saved after our baptism. As time goes by, however, too many of us are unsure of our salvation. Just as baptism was that original condition, faith and confession are ways we continue to accept salvation (Colossians 1:22-23; 1 John 1:7-9). Do you trust baptism more than the later conditions?

Our trust in self (performance) leads God to then demand perfection of us (Galatians 3:10-12). Our trust in God (his unmerited favor) allows God to accept our faith in place of perfection (Romans 1:17). The difference between legalism and faithfulness is in what we are thinking, our attitude, not what we are doing. Obedience to God's word is presupposed, but the attitudes with which we obey will make or break the actions. Two people may do the same things outwardly, but one of them be lost and the other saved—it is an issue of heart!

Paul's Own Journey

The route Paul took to arrive at his view of law and grace was, for all practical purposes, an obstacle course. From where he started, it is nearly inconceivable that he arrived where he did. He was trained at the feet of Gamaliel (Acts 22:3), well-known both inside and outside the Bible record. One would imagine that Saul must have been one of his most outstanding disciples, destined to be another Gamaliel perhaps. Paul understood the depths of legalistic Judaism. He was steeped in the most rigid form of it: Pharisaism, and in that setting was legalistically faultless (Philippians 3:6). From what we read in the NT, his zeal eclipsed everyone else's, demonstrated by his vengeful persecution of the church—what an unlikely prospect for becoming the world's premier teacher of grace!

Once Jesus appeared to him on the road to Damascus, he fasted and prayed for three days (and assumedly, nights). I suspect it took that long for him to face the fact that he and God's truth were at opposite ends of the pole. The shock to his system of belief must have been staggering! No one in the world was more convinced that he was right than was Paul, and now he had to face the magnitude of his error and sin. The fact that Judas had contributed to the death of Jesus led him to commit suicide rather than live with the consequences of his choices. Paul, with far more courage and convictions than we might imagine, faced his future with an understanding of grace that no one else likely had—then or now. We are most blessed to sit at his feet and to drink deeply of a message that turned him into a gentle nurturer of souls instead of a violent blasphemer of disciples, a messenger of good news instead of an enforcer of legalism.

The Value of Romans

The only motivation for serving God that can last a lifetime is our love responding to his grace. Fear may get our attention (which is valid—Proverbs 1:7), but it will not keep it to the same degree that grace will. Christian fellowship may attract us at first (also valid—John 13:34-35), but it will not keep us faithful forever. Selfish ambitions, such as worldly desires for leadership positions, may motivate us to go for it for a while, but they cannot sustain us when disappointments and failures take their toll.

It has been said, "When you get Romans, God will get you!" When we really understand God's unconditional love for us, our hearts are set free to serve in a way that most religious people never fathom. We experience the difference between religion that is desire and not simply duty; religion that is delight and not drudgery; religion that is heart-deep and not simply habit-deep! God does not say, "Measure up and I will accept you," for no one ever measures up. Rather, he says, "I will accept you in Christ, and now you and I will walk and work together in my strength!"

Justified—Too Good to Be True?

Once I was working on a message for a teen audience about the need to make choices for God at a young age. I was thinking about my own teen years, when I had not made the right choices and had made many choices that I regretted later. I thought about the influence I might have had on my schoolmates if I had made godly choices, and I wished that I could go back and exert this spiritual influence on my friends of long ago. As I thought about the term "justified," it occurred to me that even if I had lived one hundred times better than I did live, complete with a positive influence on others, I could not be any more right with God than I am now! To be viewed by God "just-as-if-I'd" *never* sinned is as good as it can be! (Obviously, making spiritual choices earlier would have benefited many others, and myself as well—sin leaves its consequences emotionally, even on forgiven people.) Today my standing with God is absolutely right—*perfect* in the blood of the Lamb! This sounds too good to be true, doesn't it? It is indescribably good and altogether true, and understanding these things should change radically our way of looking at God and at our lives for him.

So let's go get Romans, and let God forever get us!

1

IIIIIIIIIIIIIIIIII

Paul's Passion and Secular Sinfulness
Romans 1

After hearing that Romans is a book about the grace of God, much of the first three chapters may prove shocking. Once Paul makes his introductions, which are full of grace, he proceeds to condemn sin with a carefully crafted forcefulness. If we are taken aback by Paul's approach, it is likely due to the influence upon our thinking of our society's lack of convictions about sin. Many find themselves in the position of wanting to see God as a totally beneficent being, incapable of administering judgment against us poor, weak humans. Yet on the other hand, their consciences still plague them with feelings of guilt. What gives, with this conflicting dichotomy? Just this: until we see our sins as God does, take full responsibility for them and then repent, we can never be set free. Understood in this light, the beginning of Romans makes perfect sense. Grace cannot be grace until sin is adequately understood. With these thoughts in mind, we can proceed into the text.

Called by Grace (Romans 1:1-7)

> [1:1]Paul, a servant of Christ Jesus, called to be an apostle and set apart for the gospel of God—[2]the gospel he promised beforehand through his prophets in the Holy Scriptures [3]regarding his Son, who as to his human nature was a descendant of David, [4]and who through the Spirit of holiness was declared with power to be the Son of God by his resurrection from the dead: Jesus Christ our Lord. [5]Through him and for his name's sake, we received grace and apostleship to call people from among all the Gentiles to the obedience that comes from faith. [6]And you also are

*among those who are called to belong to Jesus Christ.
Grace and peace to you from God our Father and from the
Lord Jesus Christ.*

*[7]To all in Rome who are loved by God and called to be
saints:*

*Grace and peace to you from God our Father and from
the Lord Jesus Christ.*

Paul begins his letter to the Romans with the statement that
he was set apart for the gospel of God, and in Galatians 1:15 he
adds that God set him apart from birth. A similar statement
appears regarding Jeremiah in the Old Testament:

*"Before I formed you in the womb I knew you,
    before you were born I set you apart;
    I appointed you as a prophet to the nations."*
(Jeremiah 1:5)

Hence, Paul begins by asserting the sovereignty of God in a way
that stretches our reasoning powers to the breaking point. Are we
but pawns in the Master's hand? What was God feeling toward
Saul of Tarsus as he persecuted Christians to the point of death,
knowing all the while that Saul would soon join forces with the
very movement he hated? More generally put, if God knows what
will happen, do we really have a choice?

As the psalmist says, "All the days ordained for me were
written in your book before one of them came to be" (Psalm
139:16). God knew in advance when we would be born, when we
will die, and everything that will occur between those two events.
Yet, remarkably, he does not rob us of our own choices. We are
free moral agents, creatures of choice by God's own design, even
though he knows in advance what those choices are going to be.
He influences us for our good, but never forces us. The foreknowledge of God and the freedom of man are equally true and
inseparably joined, surely a fact beyond human understanding.

In Romans 1:3-4, Paul sets the nature of our Savior before
his readers, for we have the true gospel only when Jesus is seen to
be human and deity at the same time. He is the descendant of

David, as the Old Testament (OT) Scriptures foretold repeatedly, but he is also the Son of God. John's gospel is probably the best witness to how "Son of God" is to be defined. Study out these verses from John in this order, and you will see what I mean: John ✶ 20:30-31; 1:1-3, 14, 18; 5:18; 8:56-59; 10:25-33; 14:6-9 and 20:24-31. You will notice that when the Jewish leaders started picking up stones to kill Jesus, it was because of his claims to be deity—the Son of God.[1]

Paul ends this section in Romans 1:5-7 by showing that we too have been called—to be saints (from *hagios*, meaning simply "set apart"). This calling is through the gospel, which must be responded to by an obedient faith. Interestingly, in a book designed to dismantle the legalistic approach to salvation by works, Paul begins and ends with the statement that faith must be accompanied by obedience (Romans 1:5, 16:26). In both passages, the literal meaning is "faith's obedience." There is one kind of obedience that belongs to faith and another type that belongs to legalistic works. The apostle's rejection of works is never to be interpreted as a rejection of obedience. The difference between the two kinds of obedience is the attitude with which we obey. If we trust our own goodness as we obey, it is legalistic and soul-damning; if we trust God's goodness as we obey, it is faith receiving grace. Whom do we *trust* as we obey—God or ourselves?

Indebted to Grace (Romans 1:8-17)

> [8]*First, I thank my God through Jesus Christ for all of you, because your faith is being reported all over the world.* [9]*God, whom I serve with my whole heart in preaching the gospel of his Son, is my witness how constantly I remember you* [10]*in my prayers at all times; and I pray that now at last by God's will the way may be opened for me to come to you.*
>
> [11]*I long to see you so that I may impart to you some spiritual gift to make you strong—*[12]*that is, that you and I may be mutually encouraged by each other's faith.* [13]*I do not want you to be unaware, brothers, that I planned many times to come to you (but have been prevented from doing so until now) in order that I might have a harvest among you, just as I have had among the other Gentiles.*

> *[14]I am obligated both to Greeks and non-Greeks, both to the wise and the foolish. [15]That is why I am so eager to preach the gospel also to you who are at Rome.*
>
> *[16]I am not ashamed of the gospel, because it is the power of God for the salvation of everyone who believes: first for the Jew, then for the Gentile. [17]For in the gospel a righteousness from God is revealed, a righteousness that is by faith from first to last, just as it is written: "The righteous will live by faith."*

One of Paul's purposes in the first chapter is evident: he had not been to Rome yet, and he wanted to express his concern for the church. His enemies had maligned his motives and slandered him repeatedly, and the Roman church had likely heard some of these things. Thus, he states his gratitude for them, shown by his prayers in their behalf and assures them that their reputation of faith has reached all over the world and is much appreciated. His failure to visit the church in the capital city was not due to a lack of desire, but to some unmentioned hindrances. His enemies had probably claimed otherwise.

In Romans 1:11 Paul mentions his desire to impart some spiritual gift to them, which may relate to how the church was originally established. When an apostle visited a church new to him or if he had established it in the first place, he could lay hands on the members in order to impart the miraculous gifts of the Holy Spirit (Acts 8:17). Rome was likely started by those converted in Jerusalem on the day of Pentecost (see Acts 2:10-11). If true, you would expect that miraculous gifts would be in short supply, being limited to those on whom the apostles had laid their hands back in Jerusalem. A comparison of the gifts mentioned in Romans 12 and 1 Corinthians 12 supports this view. In the Corinthian church, which Paul had personally established, the gifts were mostly miraculous in nature. In Romans 12, a very similar passage to 1 Corinthians 12, the gifts are nearly all nonmiraculous. His visit would have provided them with the other type of gifts, which were very needed in that first century setting.[2]

Roman 1:13 tells us that Paul lived to bring in a harvest. The following verse informs us that he felt a deep obligation to share with the lost in Rome. If a person who had cancer discovered the cure for this dreaded malady, he would be no doubt overjoyed about his own cure, but he would also feel a deep sense of obligation to share this cure with as many people as possible. Truly sin is a more dreadful disease than physical cancer—it is a cancer of the soul, ruining lives in both time and in eternity! How deeply do you feel your obligation to share this cure in Christ? Paul was *eager* to preach, not coerced or pressured to do it (v15). Further, he was unashamed of the only lasting good news in the world (v16). Jesus warns us of the seriousness of being ashamed of him and his message:

> *"If anyone is ashamed of me and my words in this adulterous and sinful generation, the Son of Man will be ashamed of him when he comes in his Father's glory with the holy angels."* (Mark 8:38)

Romans 1:17 tells why Paul was so inwardly motivated: his righteousness came from God, not his own deeds. This provided him with the ultimate motivation, described emphatically in 1 Corinthians 15:10 with these words:

> *But by the grace of God I am what I am, and his grace to me was not without effect. No, I worked harder than all of them—yet not I, but the grace of God that was with me.*

How much are you motivated by grace to share your faith?

The well-known theme of Romans is found in 1:16-17. The gospel is full of power, from *dunamis*, the Greek word from which our words "dynamite" and "dynamo" come. This power can save us originally and then keep us saved with *salvation* grace, and it can continue to change us into Christ's likeness with *strengthening* grace! Grace was never intended to just cover our sins (though thankfully it does that), but to empower us to grow stronger and stronger in our rejection of Satan's temptations. Paul charged Timothy to "be strong in the grace that is in Christ Jesus" (2 Timothy 2:1). The more we appreciate grace, the more we hate sin in our lives.

The "righteousness from God" in Romans 1:17 refers to the manner in which God makes men righteous by enabling them to participate in his own righteousness. We are all clearly unrighteous in our sins, but when we are baptized into Christ, we are clothed with God's righteousness (Galatians 3:26-27). Praise God! I may not be all that I need to be, but I am not what I used to be! The quote in Romans 1:17 from the Old Testament comes from Habakkuk 2:4. In its original context, God was reminding the prophet that trusting God no matter what the circumstances provided the only answer to the complexities and problems of life. Once the prophet internalized this principle, he penned these amazing words in Habakkuk 3:17-18:

> *Though the fig tree does not bud*
> *   and there are no grapes on the vines,*
> *though the olive crop fails*
> *   and the fields produce no food,*
> *though there are no sheep in the pen*
> *   and no cattle in the stalls,*
> *yet I will rejoice in the Lord,*
> *   I will be joyful in God my Savior.*

Therefore, let's pray that our study of Romans brings us the joy and confidence of Habakkuk and his later brother, Paul—the prophets of the *heart set free*!

Exposed by Grace (Romans 1:18-32)

> [18]*The wrath of God is being revealed from heaven against all the godlessness and wickedness of men who suppress the truth by their wickedness,* [19]*since what may be known about God is plain to them, because God has made it plain to them.* [20]*For since the creation of the world God's invisible qualities—his eternal power and divine nature— have been clearly seen, being understood from what has been made, so that men are without excuse.*
> [21]*For although they knew God, they neither glorified him as God nor gave thanks to him, but their thinking became futile and their foolish hearts were darkened.* [22]*Although they claimed to be wise, they became fools* [23]*and exchanged the glory of the immortal God for images made to look like mortal man and birds and animals and reptiles.*

24Therefore God gave them over in the sinful desires of their hearts to sexual impurity for the degrading of their bodies with one another. 25They exchanged the truth of God for a lie, and worshiped and served created things rather than the Creator—who is forever praised. Amen.

26Because of this, God gave them over to shameful lusts. Even their women exchanged natural relations for unnatural ones. 27In the same way the men also abandoned natural relations with women and were inflamed with lust for one another. Men committed indecent acts with other men, and received in themselves the due penalty for their perversion.

28Furthermore, since they did not think it worthwhile to retain the knowledge of God, he gave them over to a depraved mind, to do what ought not to be done. 29They have become filled with every kind of wickedness, evil, greed and depravity. They are full of envy, murder, strife, deceit and malice. They are gossips, 30slanderers, God-haters, insolent, arrogant and boastful; they invent ways of doing evil; they disobey their parents; 31they are senseless, faithless, heartless, ruthless. 32Although they know God's righteous decree that those who do such things deserve death, they not only continue to do these very things but also approve of those who practice them.

Before we are ready to appreciate and accept the good news of the gospel, we must first be convicted of the bad news: our own sinfulness! The Holy Spirit came to convict the world first of sin, righteousness and judgment, not of grace (John 16:7-8). Note how the Spirit did exactly that in Acts 2, especially in verses 36-40. Similarly, note the wording of Acts 24:25: "Paul discoursed on righteousness, self-control and the judgment to come." The message of Romans 1:18-3:20 is not "How can a loving God send anyone to hell?" Rather, it is "How can a just God not send *everyone* to hell"! The seriousness of sin and its consequences are seldom understood by anyone for long, for Satan works mightily to water down our view of it.

Romans 1:18-32 makes the point abundantly clear that the non-Jewish world in Paul's time, the Gentiles, were lost in sin. Consequently, regardless of anyone's background and religious training, he is accountable to God (1:18-20). This accountability traces back to the voice of conscience. We may suppress the truth it brings to light for us, but we know better deep inside. To assuage our smitten consciences, we approve of others doing the same sinful things (Romans 1:32).

Man's accountability also traces back to the voice of creation, for the created universe shouts out the existence of God. See Psalm 19:1-4 for a beautiful depiction of this universal message. Creation demands a Creator; design demands a Designer; the effect demands a Cause! For every *classical* atheist who claims that there is no God, no Creator, there are scores of *practical* atheists who live as if there is no God. Paul's point is that man's view of God determines the progression of sin (Romans 1:21-32). The path away from God begins with a loss of thankfulness (v21). Next, humanism follows—the belief that man not only *has* the answers, he *is* the answer!

A startling concept is taught here in Romans 1, namely that God can reach the point of giving sinful man up to go his own way. In fact, the phrase that God "gave them over" is used three times in this brief section (vv24, 26, 28). This point is illustrated by the fact that a spiritual hardening can cause people to think that sexual immorality should be accepted as normal (v24-25). Once God is taken out of the picture, the strength of the sexual drive naturally leads into its misuse and abuse. Sexual perversion comes next (vv26-27). It cannot be argued in context that the "due penalty" in verse 27 is a direct reference to AIDS, but it could certainly be included as one manifestation of the principle at work. Man cannot set aside God's moral laws without paying a price for it—physically, emotionally and spiritually.

Homosexuality is called a "perversion" here and is clearly condemned in the rest of the Bible. Leviticus 18:22 and 20:13 also call such behavior a perversion. Other important New Testament (NT) passages about immorality and homosexuality are 1 Corinthians 6:9-10; 1 Timothy 1:9-10 and 2 Peter 2:14-15. In the 1 Corinthians 6 passage, sexual sins are very specifically denoted. "Immorality" is from the Greek word *porneia*, a broad term for sexual activity outside the marriage relationship, whether before or after marriage. "Adultery" is from *moicheia*, which refers to sexual activity in an illicit relationship with at least one of the parties being married. "Male prostitutes" is from *malakos*, translated "effeminate" in the New American Standard Version, perhaps referring to the more passive partner in a homosexual relationship. "Homosexual offenders" would then most likely be the more dominant partners in a sexual act with another of their same sex.

The common justification for homosexuality is that people are born as homosexuals. Even if we grant that we are born with some strong tendencies (such as the tendency to have a hot temper, a self-focus or any one of a number of other tendencies), we are still responsible for bringing those tendencies under the control of Christ. Tendencies may define the *nature* of a person's struggle against sin, but they cannot define the *outcome* of it. In 1 Timothy 1:9-10, the word "perverts" is a reference to the practice of sodomy. In the 2 Peter passage, the consuming nature of immorality is described with the phrase, "eyes full of adultery." This provides a very accurate description of a large segment of our society today. Bottom line, they have sex on their minds, and with no reliance on God's direction and control, it colors much of their thought processes.

Excursus: Dealing with Our Sexuality

When much of our relating to the opposite sex has had sexual overtones, a number of hindrances may develop, even in the body of Christ. Lustful thoughts toward one another can be a problem. Hugs and other demonstrations of affection can cause feelings of uneasiness until we grow in this area. We may project a flirtatious spirit without being fully aware of it. Warmth is a wonderful thing, but it must be holy warmth! On the other side of the coin, mistrust of others' motives can arise because we read our former motives into their attitudes or actions (and we may well be far off base). In short, we just have to learn how to relate to the opposite sex in the way that Jesus did—as close spiritual friends. And we must avoid judging others' motives on the basis of what our own motives were in the world.

The approach to changing these worldly hindrances is not complicated. Be open with God and with others about what is really going on inside your heart and mind. Be blatantly honest with both God and others—Satan cannot thrive in the light. (Study John 3:19-21.) Avoid circumstances that would play into your present weaknesses. Keep asking for much advice about relating to the opposite sex, and then follow it. Pray for a change of mind and heart, and it will come.

Finally, the text tells us that people ultimately become depraved in all aspects of mind and behavior (vv28-32). But in spite of the depth of their depravity, they still know that what they are doing is wrong. This inner awareness of conscience motivates them to approve of others' sins, feeling that there is somehow safety in numbers, and if everyone is thinking and doing what they are, then they reason that God will have to make allowances. You might ask those in Noah's generation about that!

In this latter section, more than twenty types of sins are listed. Although the Bible identifies numerous specific sins, they can be categorized into several broad (and practical) categories. Sexual sins, as just described, grow out of our typically strong sexual awareness and drive when not handled spiritually. Likely, our biggest additional temptations fall into the headings of materialism, selfishness and pride. Note what Romans 1 and related passages can teach us about these three areas.

Materialism

In Romans 1, two of the sins listed relate directly to the overall problem of materialism: greed and envy (v29). In 2 Timothy 3:2, the people are described as "lovers of money." One of the best places in the Bible to learn about materialism is from the Gospel of Luke. This book was written to a Gentile audience with a major emphasis on the subject of repentance. It often deals specifically with the subject of money.

Someone said that the tragedy of our day is that we love things and use people, rather than loving people and using things. Loving things has a huge impact on our relationships in a number of ways. We may spend too much time trying to make money to buy more possessions, and we often spend too much time thinking about them. Our misconceptions about what will make us happy interfere with the focus we need to have on other people. "If I just had 'X,' then I would be happy." This kind of thinking is Satan's lie. One of the worst things about possessions is that they quickly begin to possess us. They must be fixed, cleaned, painted, mowed, swept, upgraded, serviced, and on and on! The time spent on our things can be staggering if we allow it to be.

However, materialism is not easy to define. Most of us define it as what the person just above our income or standard of living has. How can we tell if we are guilty of it or not? Ask yourself some probing questions. Is giving at least a tenth of your gross income a challenge to your heart? How about giving for special missions contributions—is it a duty or a delight? Do you have problems with envy toward those who have more than you? Are you uptight when children or other people appear to somehow threaten the condition of your possessions? What do you possess right now that would be very difficult to part with? Where would you *not* be willing to move, or how would you *not* be willing to live? The rich young ruler (Luke 18, Mark 10, Matthew 19) drew a line through the middle of his life and was willing to put everything over the line for God—except for one thing. Do you have such a *one thing* in your life?

Selfishness

In Romans 1, the focus on *self* was precisely the reason that most of these sins became so entrenched in the lives of the people being described. Again in 2 Timothy 3:2, Paul mentions specifically that the people were "lovers of themselves." Selfishness is one of our most pervasive sins. For this reason, Jesus started with the command to *deny* (disown) self before anything else righteous could possibly be done on anything like a consistent basis (Luke 9:23). Since the sin is so obvious, there is no need to list the multiplicity of scriptures that relate to the subject. Therefore, we will deal with the ways in which this sin manifests itself in our lives.

First, we have the sins of self-gratification—living by pleasure instead of by principle. Doing what feels good at the moment, the devil's plan, is much like our modern credit system: Buy now, pay later. With Satan, we enjoy the quick pleasures of sin, but the interest paid in heartaches lasts a long time. This approach makes us undisciplined, unorganized, unproductive, unfaithful and certainly, unfulfilled. God's plan is to pay up front with righteousness and discipline and then to enjoy tremendous dividends for a long time.

Second, we have the sin of self-justification. We rationalize our problems and sins, instead of accepting one hundred percent responsibility for what we have done and who we really are. We blame our backgrounds, our families, our circumstances and maybe even our disciplers. Yet, we are who we are because ultimately we have *chosen* it!

Third, we see the sin of self-consciousness. This *self* sin makes us very focused on what others may be thinking about us. We may imagine that people are looking at us and talking about us. We can become paranoid, believing that we are not liked and that others are even out to get us. We are afraid of people, and Satan uses our cowardice to kill our evangelism. We are insecure, which is a sin, because we are focused on ourselves rather than on God.

Fourth, we manifest the sin of self-will. The self-willed person rebels against authority, does not like seeking and following advice, and filters the direction he does receive. This sin pushes us toward comfort, materialism and greed. Therefore, when the way is too difficult, it is much easier to give up and give in.

Fifth, we can have self-pity, by feeling sorry for ourselves and working hard to evoke these same feelings in others toward us. Pity parties are commonplace, as are depression, bitterness, sarcasm and cynicism. Past hurts are magnified and massaged, as an unforgiving spirit grows stronger.

Sixth, self-protectiveness blocks a giving away of the heart and the closeness of relationships which that produces.

The damage caused by the "self" sins does not require much explanation because relationships are all about giving and not about receiving. The words of Philippians 2:1-11 are very appropriate for us in learning to refuse selfishness and to accept our responsibility to love as Jesus loved, with an unconditional commitment to the good of others, no matter what. Self-denial is the answer to all these sins of self, which means that we deny our selfish *feelings* in order to do the right things for others, just as Jesus did in the Garden of Gethsemane.

Pride

As in the case of selfishness, many of the sins in Romans 1 have their roots in pride.[3] Unlike selfishness, pride is not always so obvious. There are many types of pride and many manifestations of it in the ways we view ourselves and others. Let's look at some of these and the scriptures which relate to them.

The *types* of pride can be broken down into the pride of intellect (Romans 1:22; 1 Corinthians 1:19-29), possessions (1 Timothy 6:7-10), appearance (1 Timothy 2:9-10), social standing (James 2:1-9), race (Acts 22:21-22; Romans 2:17-24), spirituality (Luke 18:9-14) and position (Mark 10:35-45).

The *manifestations* of pride are numerous in form. It is seen in the way that we view ourselves. We may want everything our way because we are convinced that it is always the best. We may need to have our hand in everything, because no one else can do it quite as well as we can. We may need to have the last word (or last story). We may talk too much and listen too little because our opinions are so important. We may talk too little for fear that we may come across in the wrong way—this too is pride. We may take credit for everything, losing gratitude for God and others. We may see the sins of others much better than we see our own sins— or we may be *proud* of our own openness and humility! We may expect to be a special case, the exception to the rule. We may be anxiety-ridden when we cannot figure out how to get something done; then we may think that surely no one else can do it, including God himself!

In the way that we view others, pride is seen when we do not like asking for and following advice. It may grate on us to have to be submissive, *especially* to certain people. We may not like being corrected, *especially* in front of others. We may be impatient with others, *especially* if we do not think that they are as smart as we are. We may manipulate others in order to get our way because it is obviously the best way. We often may feel superior to others, and if we tend to feel inferior in some way, we find a way to tear the other person down in our own minds so that we can feel better about ourselves. We may have difficulty admitting our weaknesses and sins and making heart-felt apologies. We may have difficulty admitting our need for others and in expressing our love and appreciation for them verbally.

How does pride impact our relationships? It makes others resist us, either outwardly or inwardly. This resistance may be caused by godliness on the other person's part, for God himself resists those who are proud (1 Peter 5:5). On the other hand, the resistance may be caused by pride on the other person's part, for pride in one person often brings it out in another. Do you feel resistance to prideful people? If so, for which of the above two reasons?

Pride also keeps us from reaching out to others in order to build relationships. We are afraid that we may not be accepted by them. This fear is caused by pride. Our popular word "insecurity" is really a synonym for pride. It is commonly thought that our insecurity causes us to have a sort of defensive pride, a protective reaction. The converse is more likely the case—our pride causes us to be insecure. Most people whose insecurities run deep are very prideful, for the two usually track together. However, I can think of some very insecure people who were actually quite humble. With such exceptions in mind, the "I'm just insecure" excuse for pride falls flat on its face.

Pride damages relationships in dozens of ways. In the New International Version, there are sixty-one references to pride. In order to get the full impact of the damage that pride causes us and others in our lives, look up these passages and apply them to your life. As you do it, ask God to help you see yourself as you really are, and then to give you the will and strength become into a humble person.

✠

So what is the message of Romans 1? It is the introduction of God's grace into an atmosphere of utter degradation, brought about by a world who had forgotten God. True, man had not plummeted to the depths of the Noahic generation, when "every inclination of the thoughts of his heart was only evil all the time" (Genesis 6:5), but the world was clearly headed in that direction. No wonder Paul was so urgent to spread the gospel all over the globe.

Our present world is characterized by the same kinds of sins, and we must have the same kind of urgency. God will not tolerate indefinitely the magnitude of sins present in our society without bringing his judgment against it. As one sage put it, "If God doesn't punish America for her sins, he is going to owe an apology to Sodom and Gomorrah." This is a sobering thought, isn't it? Let's make sure that we do not simply condemn sin; let's offer the world the only hope. If Paul and the Christians in the first century significantly changed their world, we can change ours. But to do that, we must avoid the pitfalls of simply being religious, and Romans 2 will address that concern.

Notes

1. For a more in depth treatment of the Biblical claims of Christ's deity, see *Prepared to Answer*, chapter 11, which addresses the Jehovah's Witness' claims to the contrary (Billerica, Mass.: Discipleship Publications International, 1998).

2. For an in-depth study of miraculous gifts, see chapters 16-28 in *The Spirit* by Douglas Jacoby (Billerica, Mass.: Discipleship Publications International, 1998).

3. See *The Prideful Soul's Guide to Humility*, by Jones and Fontenot, for a great treatment of the subject (Billerica, Mass.: Discipleship Publications International, 1998).

2

Religious Sinfulness
Romans 2

After exposing the sinfulness of the Gentile world in the first chapter of Romans, Paul quickly moves on to the sinfulness of the Jews in chapter 2. Being religious is not the same as being spiritual or even as being right with God, contrary to popular opinion—then and now. By the time a good first century Jew had finished reading Romans 1, he surely must have been thinking, "Preach on, Brother Paul. You are exactly right about those ungodly pagans!" However, as he kept reading, that smug, self-righteous smile must have been wiped off his face by Paul's totally unexpected conclusion: Jews are no more pleasing to God than the Gentiles; and in fact, they may be less pleasing!

Jewish Subtle Sinfulness (Romans 2:1-4)

> [2:1] *You, therefore, have no excuse, you who pass judgment on someone else, for at whatever point you judge the other, you are condemning yourself, because you who pass judgment do the same things. [2] Now we know that God's judgment against those who do such things is based on truth. [3] So when you, a mere man, pass judgment on them and yet do the same things, do you think you will escape God's judgment? [4] Or do you show contempt for the riches of his kindness, tolerance and patience, not realizing that God's kindness leads you toward repentance?*

The Jews (religious types) practiced essentially the same sins as the irreligious, except with more subtlety. In his Sermon on the Mount, Jesus had earlier addressed what amounted to a double standard when he put anger and lust into the same category as murder and adultery (Matthew 5:21-22, 27-28). We tend to think that wrong actions are far more reprehensible than wrong attitudes because the immediate consequences are more obvious and serious. But in God's sight, both are equally wrong. Hence, his condemnation of the Jewish double standard, based on their deeply ingrained self-righteousness.

Romans 2:4 shows something of the reasoning of the Jews about their righteousness. Many passages in the Old Testament promised physical and spiritual blessings when God's will was embraced. The Jews came to equate physical blessings with God's approval. In other words, if they were blessed physically, God must be pleased with them and was blessing them as a result. It is true that God does promise to take care of his followers. As David put it in Psalm 37:25, "I was young and now I am old, yet I have never seen the righteous forsaken or their children begging bread." God provides for the needs of his faithful children (but he does not promise to provide for their *wants*). However, the ability to gain money or succeed in other endeavors does not prove that God's name or his power was involved.

The Jews' convictions about this are similar to the Manifest Destiny beliefs, espoused during the settling of America, that led to the near annihilation of native Americans in many places. We may have the power to accomplish many things, but doing so does not necessarily demonstrate God's approval. Satan can "bless" us with opportunities and success—and use them to draw us away from God. Of course, whatever Satan does, God allows. In the broad sense, God allows everything that happens, good or bad. He has an ideal will (righteousness) and also an allowed will (based on man's free choices). But just because we have the freedom and ability to do something, we should not conclude that God wants us to do it. Righteousness can only be proved by what is found in the Bible. Do what it says and you will be blessed— spiritually blessed with grace and physically with what you need.

Romans 2:4 is a wonderful demonstration of God's unlimited patience (1 Timothy 1:16). In spite of horrible rebellion against God's will, God was kind to the Jewish nation far beyond what their sins deserved. Even now he causes the sunshine and rain to fall on just and unjust alike because he is kind and wants life to be good for us. His kindness toward us should not make us proud and self-sufficient, but rather humble and dependent on him. However, if his kindness does not accomplish his desires for our repentance, divine discipline is the eventual step. Even then, his goal is for us to change, not to be destroyed. Hebrews 12:5-13 is a classic passage about God's discipline, equating it with encouragement and love, but we would all agree that responding quickly to God's kindness is far better than having to later respond to his discipline.

Jewish Expectations of Partiality (Romans 2:5-16)

> [5]*But because of your stubbornness and your unrepentant heart, you are storing up wrath against yourself for the day of God's wrath, when his righteous judgment will be revealed.* [6]*God "will give to each person according to what he has done."* [7]*To those who by persistence in doing good seek glory, honor and immortality, he will give eternal life.* [8]*But for those who are self-seeking and who reject the truth and follow evil, there will be wrath and anger.* [9]*There will be trouble and distress for every human being who does evil: first for the Jew, then for the Gentile;* [10]*but glory, honor and peace for everyone who does good: first for the Jew, then for the Gentile.* [11]*For God does not show favoritism.*
>
> [12]*All who sin apart from the law will also perish apart from the law, and all who sin under the law will be judged by the law.* [13]*For it is not those who hear the law who are righteous in God's sight, but it is those who obey the law who will be declared righteous.* [14]*(Indeed, when Gentiles, who do not have the law, do by nature things required by the law, they are a law for themselves, even though they do not have the law,* [15]*since they show that the requirements of the law are written on their hearts, their consciences also bearing witness, and their thoughts now accusing, now even defending them.)* [16]*This will take place on the day when God will judge men's secrets through Jesus Christ, as my gospel declares.*

God does not show favoritism. In fact, when we know more about him, he expects more of us (Luke 12:47-48). The Gentiles had some awareness of a moral law in their hearts, for the concept of right and wrong is a part of everyone's thinking. These concepts may not be developed very well, but they are present nonetheless. All humans have that sense of "ought to." In the absence of a written law, Cain still knew that the world's first murder was wrong. Some truths are self-evident, as the framers of the U.S. Constitution accurately stated.

Moral laws come from God's nature and are, to a major extent, self-evident. Other laws come from the voice of God in revelation and are not self-evident. To state it another way, some laws are in the Bible because they are true (the moral laws), while others are true simply because they are in the Bible. The moral laws were true from the beginning, whether or not God had them written down. However, when God did inspire men to write, these types of laws were always included in that written revelation.

It should be obvious that the moral laws are easier to accept than are the others. This explains why religious people accept the Biblical teaching about stealing much more easily than the Biblical teaching about baptism. The latter requires more faith to accept.

The gist of Romans 2:12-16 is that the Gentiles had a law to which they were accountable even in the absence of written law. Since the entire thrust of chapters 1-3 is to show that everyone is under sin and lost, Paul is not arguing that the Gentiles were already right with God through a law of conscience—Romans 1 destroys that idea. He is simply showing that some Gentiles were making some response to God's moral laws even without a written revelation like the Jews had. Therefore, the Jews had no justification for looking down on the Gentiles and trying to feel better by comparison.

We often speak of "conscience," but what is it? Biblically, it is an inner voice which sits in judgment over our attitudes and actions (Romans 2:15). It is not infallible and is only as good as it is trained. Since we all receive worldly training as non-Christians, the conscience must be retrained by the Scriptures. Two vital lessons regarding the conscience must be kept in mind. One, we must always strive to keep our consciences clear before God and men (Acts 24:16; 1 Timothy 1:15, 19), while realizing that a clear conscience does not guarantee innocence (1 Corinthians 4:4).

Why not? Because our consciences can be weak (accusing us inaccurately—1 Corinthians 8:7, 10), seared over (1 Timothy 4:2), corrupted (Titus 1:15) and guilty (Hebrews 10:22).

Two, when the conscience has not been trained properly, it must not be violated in the process of retraining it (Romans 14:22-23). Although religion per se cannot clear the conscience (Hebrews 9:9), the blood of Christ, properly applied, can (Hebrews 9:14). Paul said that his truthfulness was confirmed in his conscience in the Holy Spirit (Romans 9:1). Since a clear conscience does not guarantee innocence ("it is the Lord who judges"—1 Corinthians 4:4), to be approved by the Spirit must mean that our actions or thoughts are based on the Spirit-inspired word. The real danger comes when we trust our emotions and attribute them to an inner prompting of the Holy Spirit. Emotion and conscience are not the same. Emotion can be selfishly directed, leading us to violate our consciences with the help of the rationalization process.

In making decisions, conscience should move us to be surrendered and open-minded and to get plenty of advice. Emotionalism can move us to be independent and untrusting of others. Bottom line, if you feel like making a decision without *wanting* advice, Satan is using your emotions. If you want advice in order to ensure a godly decision, God is using your conscience. This line of reasoning does not rule out prompting by the Spirit, but it does raise a proper caution. The Spirit will never prompt us in a direction that violates Biblical principles, and such prompting must be confirmed by advice from mature spiritual people (Proverbs 12:15, 13:10, 14:12, 19:20, 20:18; Romans 15:14).

Jewish Self-Righteousness (Romans 2:17-24)

> [17]Now you, if you call yourself a Jew; if you rely on the law and brag about your relationship to God; [18]if you know his will and approve of what is superior because you are instructed by the law; [19]if you are convinced that you are a guide for the blind, a light for those who are in the dark, [20]an instructor of the foolish, a teacher of infants, because you have in the law the embodiment of knowledge and truth—[21]you, then, who teach others, do you not teach

yourself? You who preach against stealing, do you steal?
²²You who say that people should not commit adultery, do
you commit adultery? You who abhor idols, do you rob
temples? ²³You who brag about the law, do you dishonor
God by breaking the law? ²⁴As it is written: "God's name is
blasphemed among the Gentiles because of you."

The nature of Jewish self-righteousness is demonstrated clearly here. Jews (especially the religious ones) were braggarts with attitudes of superiority, viewing themselves as God's gift to the world for the purpose of straightening it out. Someone has said that arrogance is the only disease that makes everyone sick except the person who has it! Not only did they think more highly of themselves than they ought to, but the Jews whom Paul addressed did not see their own sins; they were masters at rationalization. They stole in ways that seemed minor; they committed adultery in their hearts and minds; they robbed temples; they dishonored God by breaking his law in many ways.

How were they committing such sins? First, through their ancestors, whom they were so proud of. Jews worshiped their lineage, as may be evidenced by the preachers in Acts going back to the treasured history of the nation time and time again in order to build audience rapport. But by esteeming those who had committed sacrilege during the previous centuries, they found themselves accomplices to those sinners. Did not Jesus state this principle in Matthew 23:25-36? Second, through their traditions and sophistry, they in fact had robbed God (of the tithe—Malachi 3:8-10) and their parents (of needed financial support in the name of the temple—Matthew 15:3-9). Colossians 3:5 equates greed with idolatry.

Some of our most serious sins are likely the subtle, nonovert types. We may be completely oblivious to them, but rest assured that others are not. Such hypocrisy turns others away from God and causes them even to blaspheme him. When I first attended church as a young adult, the preacher told about inviting someone in the community to church. The person being invited asked the preacher if a certain man was a member there, to which the preacher answered "Yes." The man responded that if such a person was a member of that church, then he wanted no part of it. Someone has said that the reason people are not Christians is either because they have seen one (a hypocrite) or have not seen one (a true disciple). The price tag of hypocrisy is huge, Paul essentially says—and so says personal experience. Interestingly, after the preacher mentioned the above story, five men (regrettably, including me) each came to ask if he was the one being described. The one he had described never came to ask. Like a first century Jew, he evidently had rationalized himself into believing he was righteous in spite of his hypocrisy.

Jewish Trust in Their 'Official Seal' (Romans 2:25-29)

> [25]*Circumcision has value if you observe the law, but if you break the law, you have become as though you had not been circumcised.* [26]*If those who are not circumcised keep the law's requirements, will they not be regarded as though they were circumcised?* [27]*The one who is not circumcised physically and yet obeys the law will condemn you who, even though you have the written code and circumcision, are a lawbreaker.*
>
> [28]*A man is not a Jew if he is only one outwardly, nor is circumcision merely outward and physical.* [29]*No, a man is a Jew if he is one inwardly; and circumcision is circumcision of the heart, by the Spirit, not by the written code. Such a man's praise is not from men, but from God.*

Jews in Paul's day and in our day have no special place in God's plan unless they become Christians. Note what Paul says in Philippians 3:3: "For it is we who are the circumcision, we who worship by the Spirit of God, who glory in Christ Jesus, and who put no confidence in the flesh." Even a cursory reading of John's gospel should convince anyone that the physical Jew has no advantage in the sight of God. I do find the position of physical Jews who become Christians to be a special one, for they are children of Abraham in two ways: by birth and by faith. I can only claim the latter! But the modern claim that somehow Jews still have a major place in God's plans today is without Biblical substantiation, in spite of televangelists' fanciful claims to the contrary.

The first century Jews trusted their "official seal" of circumcision in a dangerous way. Being circumcised was a necessary part of God's law for them, but without righteousness following it, it was of no benefit spiritually. The circumcision with which God is most concerned, as seen in both the Old Testament and the New Testament (Deuteronomy 10:16, 30:6; Colossians 2:11-12), is that of the heart.

The confusion that existed in the Jews' minds traced back to the fact that many blessings for righteousness were bestowed on them as a nation. The nation was blessed for righteousness and cursed for unrighteousness. But the simple fact is that being a part of the nation did not ensure personal, spiritual salvation. During the OT period, two elections ran concurrently. One was the election of the nation as a whole to prepare the way for Christ's coming. The other was the election of spiritual individuals within the nation who were truly seekers and servers of God. The latter group always constituted only a *remnant* of the whole, as Paul argues forcefully in Romans 9 and 10. John the Baptist made the same point in Matthew 3:9: "And do not think you can say to yourselves, 'We have Abraham as our father.' I tell you that out of these stones God can raise up children for Abraham."

The lesson for us should be rather obvious. Those addressed by Paul were prone to trust in their "official seal" of circumcision, and some of us today are prone to trust in our "official seal" of baptism. In either case, the seal did not and cannot count unless the heart was/is circumcised! Unless our hearts are with God, we are not going to be saved.

To reiterate, Paul's argument in Romans 2 is not that somehow the Gentiles were right with God by a law of conscience. His argument is aimed at the Jews, showing that by comparison, some Gentiles were more consistent with the light that they had than were the Jews with the far greater light of Scripture.

However, it is interesting to contemplate the state of the Gentile world before the cross. It has been taught in some circles that God has dealt with mankind in three basic periods or "dispensations." First was the Patriarchal Age, when fathers were the spiritual heads of their families and served as priests for them.

This period lasted from the creation until the Law of Moses was given and included people like Abraham and his family, who were saved. Job is a good example of a father/priest during this dispensation. Second was the Mosaic Age, when the nation of Israel was governed by the Law given at Sinai. This age lasted up until the cross, when the Christian Age began for the whole world and now constitutes the only access to God for either Gentiles or Jews (John 14:6).

During the Mosaic period, the Law of Moses allowed non-Jews, Gentiles, to become a part of the nation, although they did not have all of the privileges of Jews. However, the Mosaic Law did not have a Great Commission as a part of its teaching, commanding them to go convert the Gentiles to Judaism.

So, what happened to the Gentiles during this period? We must remember that the purpose of the Old Testament was not to answer this question, but to show how God developed the Jewish nation until the coming of its Messiah to save the world. However, we do read about the repentance of the people of Nineveh when God sent Jonah to preach to them. And Balaam was a Gentile prophet who seemed to be under God's direction until his greed got the better of him. God had some dealings with the Gentile world during the Mosaic Age, it seems clear, although the exact details of it are not. It could be argued that the Patriarchal Age lasted for the Gentiles up until the time of the cross, which would allow for the possibility of some being saved during that period.

Since Jesus came, the Bible is adamant about no possibility of salvation being extended to anyone outside of Christ. Paul's comment to the Athenians supports this: "In the past God overlooked such ignorance, but now he commands all people everywhere to repent" (Acts 17:30). The ignorance of which he spoke had to do with idolatry. God seemed to cut the Gentiles more slack than he did the Jews because they had less light. Our accountability before him is based primarily on our knowledge (Luke 12:47-48), our opportunities (Galatians 6:10) and our gifts (Matthew 25:14-30). The Gentiles had less understanding, opportunities and gifts than the Jews and so were judged by a lower standard. Certainly, it is comforting to think that the masses of non-Jews during the OT period were not without the possibility of finding God. However, since Scripture does not develop this line of inquiry, it must remain merely human speculation. One thing is certain: Since the cross, no one can be right with God without faith in Christ.

We must understand why people who have never heard the gospel are lost, as difficult as it is to contemplate. If a man was drowning, and I refused to throw him a life jacket, why would he die? It would not be because I did not throw the life jacket. He would drown because he was in the water and could not swim. He failed to be *saved* (rescued) because I did not throw the life jacket. The question is often asked: "What about people who have not heard of Christ?" Men and women are not first of all lost because they have not heard of Christ. They are lost because of their sins and, consequently, have no basis for being saved. However, it is also true that they may stay lost because we do not throw them "life jackets." Sin is their problem, and they are responsible for that. But we are also responsible if we do not do all that we can to take the gospel to them!

✝

It is easy to cast stones at the self-righteous Jews, but honestly, we need to learn from them. They did have much to commend them: their belief in the God of the Bible (however faulty some parts of that view may have been); their commitment to follow what they held to be true; their Biblical view of morality in contrast to the paganism that surrounded them; their willingness to suffer through centuries of persecution; their willingness to die for what they held sacred. No one can scoff at these things. However, they lost their moorings of a true faith in God, and built a system that deceived them into thinking that they were pleasing God when they were not. Systems are easily built and certainly not easily dismantled. Do we have a system? Do you have a system? Spend some time meditating on these questions, and measure your answers against what you are learning from Romans. Keep reading and keep thinking. God will reward these efforts to dig more deeply for understanding and for faith.

3

Universal Sinfulness
Romans 3

As Paul ends his task of the first three chapters—that of showing the whole world to be under sin—he answers questions that he knew the Jews had. The first eight verses of chapter 3 fit into the arguments of chapter 2. The Jewish readers would evidently have been thinking about the implications of what Paul had written and about charges they had already heard about him and his teaching. In true Pauline fashion, Paul refuses to be governed by a conflict avoidance system, but rather by personal convictions based on God's truth. Notice how Paul reaches his conclusion of mankind's universal sinfulness.

Jewish Failure (3:1-8)

> *3:1What advantage, then, is there in being a Jew, or what value is there in circumcision? 2Much in every way! First of all, they have been entrusted with the very words of God.*
>
> *3What if some did not have faith? Will their lack of faith nullify God's faithfulness? 4Not at all! Let God be true, and every man a liar. As it is written:*
>
> > *"So that you may be proved right when you speak*
> > *and prevail when you judge."*
>
> *5But if our unrighteousness brings out God's righteousness more clearly, what shall we say? That God is unjust in bringing his wrath on us? (I am using a human argument.) 6Certainly not! If that were so, how could God judge the world? 7Someone might argue, "If my falsehood enhances God's truthfulness and so increases his glory,*

*why am I still condemned as a sinner?" ⁸Why not say—as
we are being slanderously reported as saying and as some
claim that we say—"Let us do evil that good may result"?
Their condemnation is deserved.*

If Jews were no better off than Gentiles were, what advantage
was there to being a part of the so-called "chosen people"? Good
question, but one easily answered: they had the Scriptures. It was
not God's fault that so few followed the law by faith instead of by
works. He graciously adopted the Jews as a nation when he
brought them out of Egypt, gave them his words and sent prophets
for centuries to warn them when they wandered from his words.
Surely God cannot be blamed for the unrighteousness of man. I
once knew a person who kept blaming God for allowing her to be
abused by a close relative. My reply was that God, through his
word, begged the perpetrator to refrain from such sins. Did that
person listen? No. But we cannot blame God for the consequences of the perpetrator's sins, devastating as they may be, and
we can rest assured that he will eventually pay for his misuse of
his freedom of choice.

In Romans 3:5-8, Paul answers a charge brought against him
by his critics. They claimed that if Paul's preaching was true, then
their unrighteousness enabled God's grace to shine more brightly
as he forgave their increased sin. Later, in responding to the same
accusation Paul asks, "What shall we say, then? Shall we go on
sinning so that grace may increase?" (Romans 6:1). Romans 6
deals with such thinking in detail, as we will see when we reach
that chapter. Suffice it to say that the legalist has a difficult time
understanding grace. In his thinking, grace will only cause people
to take sin lightly.

I remember an older preacher in my former denomination
who argued that we should never preach that one can be sure of
salvation because people will take advantage of it and let their
spiritual guards down. Dangling people over the fires of hell
seemed to be his best take on how to get people to heaven. He
should have changed the words of the old, popular hymn from
"Blessed Assurance" to "Cursed Assurance"—God help him!

Universal Failure (3:9-20)

> ^{9}What shall we conclude then? Are we any better? Not
> at all! We have already made the charge that Jews and
> Gentiles alike are all under sin. ^{10}As it is written:
>
> "There is no one righteous, not even one;
> ^{11}there is no one who understands,
>   no one who seeks God.
> ^{12}All have turned away,
>   they have together become worthless;
> there is no one who does good,
>   not even one."
> ^{13}"Their throats are open graves;
>   their tongues practice deceit."
> "The poison of vipers is on their lips."
> ^{14}"Their mouths are full of cursing and
>   bitterness."
> ^{15}"Their feet are swift to shed blood;
> ^{16}ruin and misery mark their ways,
> ^{17}and the way of peace they do not know."
> ^{18}"There is no fear of God before their eyes."
>
> ^{19}Now we know that whatever the law says, it says to
> those who are under the law, so that every mouth may be
> silenced and the whole world held accountable to God.
> ^{20}Therefore no one will be declared righteous in his sight by
> observing the law; rather, through the law we become con-
> scious of sin.

Paul's line of reasoning is not complex. He strings together
quotes from the Old Testament, most of which are from the
Psalms, showing the sinfulness of mankind. In Romans 3:19-20,
he drives home the point that these verses speak to those under
the law and not simply to the Gentiles. He further argues that the
law makes us conscious of sin, but cannot remove it by our flawed
obedience. Only God can do that by our faith, which he will
expound on in the next section.

The challenge ushered in by these quotes is that in their
original context, they referred to the enemies of God, not to the

righteous within the Jewish nation. For example, the quote in Romans 3:12 comes from Psalm 14:1, which reads:

> *The fool says in his heart,*
>   *"There is no God."*
> *They are corrupt, their deeds are vile;*
>   *there is no one who does good.*

How are we to understand Paul's application in this present context to all mankind? The simple answer is that the most righteous person in the world is not righteous without God's provision of forgiveness. Thus, in a practical sense, people are righteous by faith, but in the purely legal sense, without the intervention of God's grace, all are unrighteous. This reasoning certainly is true, but does not exhaust the deeper issues here.

A similar application of an OT passage is found in Galatians 3:10-12, written by Paul a number of years before Romans. A study of this passage will shed light on his reasoning in Romans 3.

> *All who rely on observing the law are under a curse, for it is written: "Cursed is everyone who does not continue to do everything written in the Book of the Law." Clearly no one is justified before God by the law, because, "The righteous will live by faith." The law is not based on faith; on the contrary, "The man who does these things will live by them." (Galatians 3:10-12)*

The quote in Galatians 3:10 is from Deuteronomy 27:26, and the quote in Galatians 3:12 is from Leviticus 18:5. In the first of these OT passages, Moses simply says that the people should faithfully follow Scripture. In the original context, Moses is not saying that the people had to perfectly obey, for that would have been impossible—they were already sinners. Rather, he is saying that they should faithfully obey. In the Leviticus passage, he is saying the same thing: be faithful to God and his word and you will live spiritually. However, Paul clearly applies the passages more rigidly than they were in their original contexts. What are we to make of this?

We get one hint in the beginning of Galatians 3:10, namely that the issue he was addressing was a reliance on observing the law instead of on the God of the law. We get another hint by comparing the quote of Galatians 3:11, also from the Old Testament (Habakkuk 2:4), to the statement in Galatians 3:12 that "the law is not based on faith." The book of Habakkuk is in the Old Testament and is quoted several times in the New Testament to demonstrate that the path to God is by faith and not by works.

Further, no one could read the book of Deuteronomy and come to the conclusion that the law is not of faith. Certainly the law was designed to be based on faith. The problem in Galatians is that those being addressed by Paul had seriously misunderstood the meaning of righteousness. They actually thought that they were righteous by their observance of the law, which made the law an end to itself, rather than a means to an end. When we use law as an instrument to express trust in God, God says, "Be faithful." When we use law as an instrument to express trust in self, he says, "Be perfect." Therefore, when the Galatians insisted on clinging to the law and their own goodness, Paul said that the law was not of faith for them. He was dealing with a perverted view and use of law, otherwise known as legalism.

Now to Romans 3 and the application of what we learned from Galatians. Because the Judaizing teachers of the first century viewed and used law incorrectly, it had for them become simply a legal system which was negative, condemning and devoid of the grace of God. But when it is viewed and used properly, law points us to the grace of God. To the humble, law is a matter of faith, since it defines our faithful response to a graceful God. To the proud upholder of religiosity, law is a matter of works, and without the grace of God, it can only be an instrument of condemnation. The negative statements in Paul's writing about law and works must be understood in this light, or we will develop erroneous understandings of both.

No matter which approach you use, the simple or the complex, the point is the same: All are under sin, Jew and Gentile alike. No one has come close to either doing good or being righteous when compared to Jesus rather than to other people. Too many have a balancing-scale view of sin, thinking that their good deeds offset their bad ones. Think about this illustration. If a man lived an exemplary life for his first forty years, then murdered a person, then changed his identity and lived forty more exemplary years, at age eighty he would still be a murderer. Neither good deeds nor the passage of time can offset a crime once committed. The laws of man do not work like that, and neither do the laws of God.

When people first begin studying the Bible with disciples, they are often shocked at the narrowness of the path to which Jesus calls us (Matthew 7:13-14, 21). Those who do not deal with their sentimentality make statements about the wonderful people in their families or churches, and have difficulty believing that they could possibly be lost. It is easy for us to feel sympathy for people whom we know, but we should feel much more sympathy for God, and hurt for him, given all that he has done to reach out to people through his crucified Son, his word and his people. To how much trouble have all of these supposedly good people gone to really search out the Word and to seek God, according to his will rather than their own? On the whole, men have not used the opportunities that they have been given, and they are therefore without excuse before God.

All men are under sin because they have fallen short of God's plan for them. The main word for sin is *hamartia* in the Greek, which comes from an archery term that means "to miss the mark." It is vital to note that the mark could be missed by both sins of commission (doing wrong things) and omission (failing to do right things). Since our mark in the NT era is the example of Jesus (1 John 2:6), we can miss our mark by doing what he did *not* do or by failing to do what he *did*. Since he did not commit sexual sins, we should be very convicted if we do commit such sins. On the other hand, since his life centered around seeking and saving the lost (Luke 19:10), we should also be very convicted if our lives are not focused in the same way. The truth is that we are often much more alarmed at the former than we are at the latter. We simply do not see life as God sees it, and we are more like the legalistic Jews than we think. Everyone needs to recognize his accountability before God because, as we can see, the best of us really is a mess!

...versal Righteousness Available (3:21-31)

> [21] But now a righteousness from God, apart from law, has been made known, to which the Law and the Prophets testify. [22] This righteousness from God comes through faith in Jesus Christ to all who believe. There is no difference, [23] for all have sinned and fall short of the glory of God, [24] and are justified freely by his grace through the redemption that came by Christ Jesus. [25] God presented him as a sacrifice of atonement, through faith in his blood. He did this to demonstrate his justice, because in his forbearance he had left the sins committed beforehand unpunished— [26] he did it to demonstrate his justice at the present time, so as to be just and the one who justifies those who have faith in Jesus.
>
> [27] Where, then, is boasting? It is excluded. On what principle? On that of observing the law? No, but on that of faith. [28] For we maintain that a man is justified by faith apart from observing the law. [29] Is God the God of Jews only? Is he not the God of Gentiles too? Yes, of Gentiles too, [30] since there is only one God, who will justify the circumcised by faith and the uncircumcised through that same faith. [31] Do we, then, nullify the law by this faith? Not at all! Rather, we uphold the law.

Once Paul fully establishes the sinful plight of mankind as a whole, he ushers in the doctrine of God's provision of grace. He summarizes the grace/faith principle in the latter part of Romans 3. Next he will demonstrate it through the example of Abraham in Romans 4. Afterward he will carefully describe the basis of the formula in Romans 5: the cross of Jesus Christ. In Romans 6, he will show how we accept grace and through dying to sin with Christ in baptism. He will demonstrate in Romans 7 the absolute misery that awaits us if we try to gain salvation any other way. Finally, in Romans 8, he will show why there is no condemnation for those who are in Christ and are walking by faith. This material contains the very heart of the book of Romans, and once we are able to absorb it at the emotional level, our lives cannot help but change. All Biblical doctrines must in some way relate to this most beautiful of all doctrines: the God who *is* love offers *himself* to his creation!

The concept of salvation by faith and not by works is introduced in capsule form in Romans 3:21-31. Verses 21-23 show the place of faith. The Old Testament pointed to this "righteousness of God," his way of making men right with himself. Since all have sinned, all can be acceptable by faith (vv22-23), for God is no respecter of persons (vv29-30). The place of grace is shown (vv24-26). Being "justified freely" (v24) gives us a beautiful picture of the completeness of God's forgiveness. "Justified" is from the Greek *dikaios,* a term with a legal background meaning to be declared "innocent" or "not guilty." The idea is not that we had our just sentences suspended or that we are out on bail or parole. We are before God simply not guilty through the blood of Christ. Therefore, God's forgiveness carries no idea of any guilt hanging over our heads at all. The word literally means *just-as-if-I'd never sinned!* Praise God for his amazing grace!

Paul proceeds to show the proper place of grace in the plan (vv24-26). Excepting Paul's greeting back in Romans 1, this passage marks the first time the word "grace" is used in the doctrinal section of Romans. Obviously, this is a very important word in the development of Paul's treatise. The Greek *charis* is found more than 170 times in the New Testament. Although it can have different shades of meaning, in Romans it denotes God's unmerited favor toward mankind. In the words of David, "He does not treat us as our sins deserve or repay us according to our iniquities" (Psalm 103:10). "Redemption" (v24) means that we have been bought back from the devil's pawnshop, the slavery of sin. In Peter's terms:

> For you know that it was not with perishable things such as silver or gold that you were redeemed from the empty way of life handed down to you from your forefathers, but with the precious blood of Christ, a lamb without blemish or defect. (1 Peter 1:18-19)

These blessings of grace are based on God's sacrifice of atonement (think "at-one-ment," being one again with God).

According to Romans 3:25, the cross showed God's justice in two related ways: one, it demonstrated that sin had to be fully paid for and not merely pushed aside; two, it righteously allowed sin to go unpunished in the lives of the faithful who lived before the cross. Until the cross, Satan could have argued, and probably did, that God was being unrighteous when he allowed people to enter paradise at death. But in the mind of a God to whom time is totally irrelevant, Jesus was already slain (1 Peter 1:20). Hebrews 9:15 also addresses this "retroactive" effect of Christ's death, mentioning that it set those under the first covenant free from their sins. In a practical sense, they were already treated as totally forgiven, but that forgiveness became legal at the cross. The Hebrew writer referred to this fact in Hebrews 11:40 as he wrote about the OT heroes of the faith: "God had planned something better for us so that only together with us would they be made perfect."

As time-bound creatures, we have difficulty understanding how God forgave before the cross. Perhaps an illustration will help. If I owe Bob one hundred dollars, he will be looking to me for payment. However, my friend Joe tells Bob, "I will pay Gordon's debt for him, but I will have to give it to you tomorrow after I go to the bank." At this point, assuming that Bob trusts Joe, he will stop looking to me for the money, even though the debt is legally not paid yet. Similarly, before the cross the faithful (those who trusted God, not their own righteousness) were forgiven for all practical purposes, but it became "official" when Jesus died.

However, the most important message in verses 24-26 is what it says about us, not what it says about men who lived before Christ. The reality of the cross allows God to accept our faith (and faithfulness) *in lieu* of perfection. Faith in the New Testament, from *pistis*, although used in somewhat different ways, most often boils down to the idea of trust. We must trust God to do for us and in us what we cannot do ourselves. Jesus is perfect and we are in a relationship with him, clothed by his perfection. We are saved not by our performance, but "through faith in his blood." When we trust not in our own efforts, but trust Jesus and the blood he shed for us, we are justified. It is *just-as-if-I'd never sinned*! When God looks at us, he sees not our flaws but Jesus' righteousness. Amazing, isn't it? Amazing grace!

Finally, the proper place of law is described in Romans 3:27-31. The law was upheld in two ways: first, its purpose of pointing to and leading the way to Christ was fulfilled; and second, by using it in its intended manner—to express our love and dependence on the only thing that can save us, God's grace. A written law from God (be it the Old Testament or the New Testament) can be used to express trust in self or in God. If the former, perfection is demanded by God (Galatians 3:6-12), and grace is ruled out. If the latter, we live in a humble yet grateful attitude, and our faithfulness is accepted instead of sinless perfection. Therefore, we are *not* under law as a means of earning our salvation (Romans 6:14), but we *are* under law as a means of walking by faith with God (1 Corinthians 9:21). The correct understanding of the distinction described above is *vital* to any person maintaining a faithful walk with God. Do not leave this section until you meditate about these two uses of law and understand the principles that have been discussed.

Keeping the proper perspective on law and grace, faith and works, is no easy matter. The avoidance of legalism is more of an art than a science, a goal neither easily achieved nor maintained. It is so easy to trust in externals instead of internals. The issue of the heart is the issue, and the heart of the issue is the heart. Without God, we are miserable sinners. As Romans 1-3 amply demonstrates, left to ourselves, the best of us is a mess. However, with God, we can be perfect in Christ, forgiven freely and enabled to become more and more like him. But this upward call of following him is not without its challenges, as the next chapters clearly show. Thankfully, the blessings are in direct proportion to the faith that we exercise in the mercy and power of God.

Now that we have been hopefully convicted of our sins and given an overview of the proper place of sin, faith and law, we stand ready to dig even deeper into God's gold mine of grace.

II

Righteousness Comes by Grace

4

Righteousness in Abraham
Romans 4

Romans 4 shows how salvation by grace through faith was demonstrated in Abraham's life. Any Jew would have said that Abraham was the father of the faithful, an outstanding example of a servant of God from almost any vantage point. He also would have said that his greatness tied in to his obedience to the covenant of circumcision, because it was at that point that he became the first real Jew. Paul will demonstrate the fallacy of this argument and show that Abraham was right with God long before being circumcised. No doubt his reasoning was a challenge to the typical Jewish viewpoint, for as shown in Romans 3, the Jews definitely trusted in that official seal of the covenant. In the end, Paul proves that Abraham had amazing faith and shows how he appropriated the saving grace of God in his life.

How Was Abraham Justified Before God? (Romans 4:1-8)

> *4:1 What then shall we say that Abraham, our forefather, discovered in this matter? 2If, in fact, Abraham was justified by works, he had something to boast about—but not before God. 3What does the Scripture say? "Abraham believed God, and it was credited to him as righteousness."*
>
> *4Now when a man works, his wages are not credited to him as a gift, but as an obligation. 5However, to the man who does not work but trusts God who justifies the wicked, his faith is credited as righteousness. 6David says the same thing when he speaks of the blessedness of the man to whom God credits righteousness apart from works:*
>
> *7"Blessed are they*
> *whose transgressions are forgiven,*

> *whose sins are covered.*
> [8]*Blessed is the man*
> *whose sin the Lord will never count against*
> *him."*

Note that the contrast that Paul makes is between works and faith, *not* obedience and faith. Abraham was in no way justified by the "works" under discussion. He did nothing to earn or merit his standing with God. The Bible uses the term "works" in two quite different ways: "works of law" and "works of faith." The essential difference between the two is in the attitude and heart of the worker. The issue is whom the worker is trusting—self or God. So, Paul argues that Abraham was not saved as a result of earning his standing by works of law, although Scripture often affirms his works of faith, which grew out of his trust in God. As is often stated, we work not in order to *be* saved, but because we *are* saved. This difference may seem subtle, but it is not. As shocking as it may seem to us, two people can do the same things outwardly, and yet, one can end up in hell while the other ends up in heaven. We need to ask ourselves whether we trust the works themselves or the God for whom we should lovingly be doing the works.

When you compare Romans 4 with James 2:21-24, it appears at first glance that the passages contradict one another. The more literal translation of the passage in James can be found in the New American Standard Version:

> *Was not Abraham our father justified by works, when he offered up Isaac his son on the altar? You see that faith was working with his works, and as a result of the works, faith was perfected; and the Scripture was fulfilled which says, "And Abraham believed God, and it was reckoned to him as righteousness," and he was called the friend of God. You see that a man is justified by works, and not by faith alone.*

In James, we are told that Abraham was justified by works. Paul, in Romans 4, says what appears to be the exact opposite. To compound the problem, both passages quote Genesis 15:6 as the proof of Abraham's justification. The apparent contradiction (*not* by works, *by* works) has caused confusion to Biblical scholars whose theology is already confused on the subject of salvation. For example, Martin Luther denied that James should even be in the Bible, calling it "an epistle of straw." However, the apparent contradiction is solved when we realize that Abraham was not justified by works (of law), but he was justified by works (of faith). The former type of works expresses dependence on self, while the latter type expresses dependence on God. Paul, writing to one audience to meet one need, referred to the former and James, writing to a different audience with an entirely different need, referred to the latter.

A part of the confusion about these seeming different uses of the term "justification" occurs because some wrongly assume that Genesis 15:6 is describing Abraham's original salvation. Some writers assert that Paul is talking about initial salvation and James about continuing salvation, but this does not solve the dilemma. Most often the Scriptures use "justification" in reference to original salvation and "sanctification" in reference to continuing salvation. However, this is not an absolute rule. In 1 Corinthians 6:11, "sanctified" is used to refer to original salvation, and in both Romans 4 and James 2, "justified" refers to continuing salvation.

Actually, we do not know when Abraham was originally saved. When the Bible reader is first introduced to Abraham, this father of the faithful is already an obedient follower of God (Genesis 12:4, 17:5; Hebrews 11:8). Therefore, "justification by faith" is the initial and continual process ("from first to last," as stated in Romans 1:17) and comes about as we show our faith in God, our trust in his promises and our obedience to his commands. Abraham trusted the promises of Genesis 15 and obeyed the commands of Genesis 22 in offering Isaac, as quoted in James 2. In both cases, he was justified by faith, and in neither case did he attempt to be justified by legalistic works.

Walking in the Light

According to Romans 4:6-8, the justified person never has his sins counted against him. Just who is the "blessed" person? The one who walks in the light (1 John 1:1-7), the one who is *in* (a relationship with) Christ, where there is "no condemnation" (Romans 8:1). It is true that a person can become "out" of Christ

again and be lost (James 1:13-15), but he should not and will not if
✱ he truly understands the grace of God and keeps responding to it.

What is "walking in the light"? Whatever this phrase means,
it *cannot* mean perfection or sinlessness. Otherwise, there would
be no sins of which to be cleansed (1 John 1:7). The verb "puri-
fies" here denotes a continual action. Just as windshield wipers
continually wipe away water, the blood of Christ continually takes
away our sins and keeps us saved. As blood in our physical
bodies continually removes impurities from our systems, Christ's
blood constantly removes impurities from those in his spiritual
body, the church.

"Walking in the light" suggests a faithful and consistent walk
with God. The unrighteous person follows Satan consistently and
will end up with him, even though he occasionally turns aside
from that path and does good. The righteous person follows Christ
consistently and will end up with him, even though he occasionally turns aside from that path and does evil. The real issue is
faithfulness—the heart and the overall outcome of one's life. None
of us is *perfect*, but any of us can be *faithful*. The difference
between faithfulness and perfection can be illustrated by asking
my wife if I am a *perfect* husband—definitely "No." On the other
hand, if asked whether I am a *faithful* husband, she would say
definitely, "Yes!"

James 1:13-15 is an important passage in showing the possibility of falling from grace and how that may occur. Although it is
possible to fall from grace, we do not play "hopscotch," jumping in
and out of grace as we sin and then repent. Years ago, I heard of a
woman who nearly had a head-on collision with a huge truck and
afterward was terrified because she thought that she was going to
die without the opportunity to pray and ask for forgiveness. She
definitely had the "hopscotch" concept of grace. Since most of us
will die between prayers, we had better figure this out now!

A clear and logical progression may be seen in James 1:13-15.
It begins with having wrong *desires*, even in Christ. These desires
then conceive and bear a baby called sin. If and when the baby
matures, it then produces death spiritually and we leave our standing in Christ. But notice that *sin* does not immediately bring
death—it must first become full-grown or mature. Between the

initial stage and the latter stage, God patiently works to get us back on track in a given area. Therefore, while we can fall from grace, it is not really as easy as some seem to feel—praise God!

I've heard the story of a man who was crossing an unfamiliar, frozen river alone one night. Fearful of falling through the ice, he moved slowly and cautiously. When he was near the middle of the river, he began to hear a strange noise and to feel vibrations. Assuming that the ice was breaking up and flowing downriver, he lay flat on the ice to spread his weight over a larger surface. He lay there with his heart pounding, terrified. As the noise grew louder and the vibrations stronger, he soon saw in the moonlight a sleigh full of people pulled by six horses going down the middle of the river. The ice was far thicker than he had dreamed. Is God's "ice" of grace thick or thin in your mind?

Great Illustration

Similarly, two workers fell to their deaths in the early days of constructing the famous Golden Gate bridge. The other workers refused to continue working until a safety net was built under their work area. The construction of the net cost the company much in time and money—or at least that is what the owners first thought. However, after the net was in place, no one ever fell again, and the work was finished well ahead of schedule, which more than made up the money and time spent. Surely the spiritual application is obvious. While grace is much more than a safety net, we can see that if we live in fear, we will be uptight, unhappy and ineffective. If we understand and trust grace, we are free to work happily and productively. Just how happy are you in your walk with the Lord?

When Was Abraham Justified? (Romans 4:9-15)

> [9]*Is this blessedness only for the circumcised, or also for the uncircumcised? We have been saying that Abraham's faith was credited to him as righteousness.* [10]*Under what circumstances was it credited? Was it after he was circumcised, or before? It was not after, but before!* [11]*And he received the sign of circumcision, a seal of the righteousness that he had by faith while he was still uncircumcised. So then, he is the father of all who believe but have not been circumcised, in order that righteousness might be credited to them.* [12]*And he is also the father of the*

circumcised who not only are circumcised but who also walk in the footsteps of the faith that our father Abraham had before he was circumcised.

[13]It was not through law that Abraham and his offspring received the promise that he would be heir of the world, but through the righteousness that comes by faith. [14]For if those who live by law are heirs, faith has no value and the promise is worthless, [15]because law brings wrath. And where there is no law there is no transgression.

The "justification" here refers to that which was previously discussed, from Genesis 15:6. In light of our earlier explanation, we know that *original* justification was not the ultimate consideration, but since the Jews tried to tie in circumcision to a person's salvation, the Genesis 15 account makes Paul's point perfectly. Abraham clearly was justified long *before* he was circumcised, so he was not justified by virtue of being a Jew nor by virtue of law keeping. Therefore, he could be the father of all the faithful—Jew and Gentile—but only to those Jews who walked in the footsteps of the faith Abraham had before circumcision. Many Jews must have winced when they read that line. In Galatians 3 and 4, Paul makes the same point, but perhaps even more forcefully. It would be good to read those chapters before proceeding further.

In Romans 4:15, Paul refers to law as a legal system without the intervention of God's grace. As such, it brings only wrath. Any law only points out the transgression of that law; it has no ability to forgive that transgression—and no amount of good deeds can offset the transgression. Just imagine that I ran a traffic light and a policeman pulled me over and started writing a violation ticket. In trying to find grace, suppose I made this plea: "Officer, I realize that I may have gone through a red light, but you need to understand something of my previous driving record. I have never run a red light in my life. Why, I must have stopped at a million red lights, and even a few green ones just for good measure. In view of that rather amazing record, I am sure that you agree that I am not guilty." All the obedience in the world does not offset one instance of disobedience, whether we are considering the law of man or the law of God. Law, without God's grace, can only point out sin and therefore condemn. If anyone understands that principle, he would never appeal to his works for justification, but the self-right-eous Jews had a difficult time understanding this.

Why Is Abraham the Example of One Justified? (Romans 4:16-25)

> [16]*Therefore, the promise comes by faith, so that it may be by grace and may be guaranteed to all Abraham's off-spring—not only to those who are of the law but also to those who are of the faith of Abraham. He is the father of us all.* [17]*As it is written: "I have made you a father of many nations." He is our father in the sight of God, in whom he believed—the God who gives life to the dead and calls things that are not as though they were.*
>
> [18]*Against all hope, Abraham in hope believed and so became the father of many nations, just as it had been said to him, "So shall your offspring be."* [19]*Without weakening in his faith, he faced the fact that his body was as good as dead—since he was about a hundred years old—and that Sarah's womb was also dead.* [20]*Yet he did not waver through unbelief regarding the promise of God, but was strengthened in his faith and gave glory to God,* [21]*being fully persuaded that God had power to do what he had promised.* [22]*This is why "it was credited to him as right-eousness."* [23]*The words "it was credited to him" were written not for him alone,* [24]*but also for us, to whom God will credit righteousness—for us who believe in him who raised Jesus our Lord from the dead.* [25]*He was delivered over to death for our sins and was raised to life for our jus-tification.*

Abraham was qualified as the father of all of the faithful not just because he was saved before circumcision, but because of the depth and consistency of his faith. He had a true hope that was devoid of humanism. Against humanistic hope, he in spiritual hope believed! He faced the facts, but he believed the promises of God in spite of the facts. In essence, he *faced* the facts and then he *faithed* the facts! For us, the fact is that we deserve eternal death. The promise is that we can be justified by grace through faith. Therefore, faith for the disciple is not realism, nor is it simply the worldly quality of optimism. Faith is actually idealism: the childlike (Matthew 18:3) decision to believe that because of Jesus' death and resurrection, our future really is as bright as the promises of God.

Abraham's faith was such a high-water mark in history that we will take the time to have a more detailed look at it. Abraham is called "father of the faithful" for good reason. He had a faith by which all others are measured and tested. Hebrews 11:8-19 lists a number of occasions when Abraham submitted to the will of God with a trust that surpassed his experiences. Actually, faith on our part is never totally blind faith—God always gives us some evidences for our faith. But then, in spite of the evidences, he will push us to our limit and demand a "leap of faith." He provided Abraham with experiences which built his faith, but then he called Abraham to make some quantum leaps of faith.

The story begins with God's call to Abram to leave his relatives and homeland. He "obeyed and went," according to Hebrews 11:8, indicating an obedient heart behind his obedient actions. He surrendered his desire to know what lay ahead. With no travel plan, no time schedule, no hotels reserved, and no housing secured in the town of his undisclosed future residence, Abraham obeyed and went. We speak of disciples being willing to go anywhere, do anything, and give up everything. It's a nice statement, but Abraham was more than willing to do those things—he did them *repeatedly* for 100 years (from the time God called him at age seventy-five until he died at 175).

Abraham was also surrendered materially. He lived in tents, rather than in a nice house, and convinced his wife to accept that same lifestyle. When the herds had grown too large for him and Lot to remain together, he gave Lot the choice of the best land. Conversely, many so-called Christians operate their business ventures with the philosophy of "God helps those who help themselves," as they grasp for complete control. The father of the faithful put the matter in a younger man's hands, trusting that his future was really in God's hands. As Hebrews 11:10 says, "He was looking forward to the city with foundations, whose architect and builder is God." A materialistic man he was not. Although God blessed him with wealth, he would have given it up in a moment.

Abraham also was surrendered in family matters (vv19-20). When God informed him that his descendants would be as numerous as the stars of heaven, he believed it, in spite of his advanced age. The timing was in God's hands. He waited on the Lord, Sarah became pregnant, and the son of promise finally made his appearance.

In my mind, the apex of Abraham's faith came some years later when God commanded him to sacrifice this beloved son. In Genesis 22:3, it says "early the next morning" Abraham set out on his journey to kill Isaac. Amazing! If I had been he, I would have postponed the whole process as long as possible. But not Abraham. He searched for reasons to trust God. In our logical humanism, we often look for reasons *not* to trust. Note in Hebrews 11:19 that "Abraham reasoned that God could raise the dead, and figuratively speaking, he did receive Isaac back from death." The Bible does not call his response "faith" specifically, because Biblical faith is based on the word of God (Romans 10:17), and in this instance, God did not tell him what the ultimate plan was.

However, Abraham clung to two fundamental truths from God. One, he knew Isaac was the son of promise through whom his lineage would multiply. Two, he knew God had commanded his death. From a human perspective, the situation made no sense at all. A sermon based on this event could be titled "When God Contradicts God." But Abraham reasoned with a childlike trust that he would kill his son, and then God would simply raise him from the dead. In spite of the monumental challenge of killing one's own son, the man took it in stride because nothing in his life was held back from God. His surrender was absolute. The Lord's verdict in the matter? "Now I know that you fear God, because you have not withheld from me your son, your only son" (Genesis 22:12). James added this postscript to the record about Abraham: "...and he was called God's friend" (James 2:23).[1]

✝

We all need heroes, and Abraham is one of my favorites. Thankfully, God tells us enough about Abe's foibles to remind us that he was human, but this in some ways raises the standard of faith even higher. Although he told a lie or two, and accepted his wife's substitute plan for gaining a son, he rose to the occasion demanded by faith time and time again, in youth and in old age.

Interestingly, in Genesis 26:5 God describes Abraham's faith with terms that seem to contradict the wording of Romans 4, even more than James 2 appears to do: "Abraham obeyed me and kept my requirements, my commands, my decrees and my laws." Clearly, this father of the faithful well understood how to view and respond to God's demands of obedience. He did what the Jews of the first century had failed to do: follow God with a sense of his own unworthiness and God's worthiness, while maintaining absolute assurance that only God could make his dreams come true. Lord, grant us that same heart and the life of trust that grows out of it!

Note

1. This material on Abraham was adapted from my book *The Victory of Surrender—Second Edition* (Billerica, Mass.: Discipleship Publications International, 1999) 93-94.

5

Righteousness Through Christ
Romans 5

In Romans 5, God's grace is shown to be free, but certainly not cheap, for it demanded a cross. This chapter contains some of the book's loftiest depictions of grace, but it also contains one of the most problematic passages in the entire Bible. As we dig into Romans 5, let's focus on the former and not become preoccupied with the latter. Difficult passages are good to grapple with, but in a book like Romans, we cannot afford to miss the central emphases. Paul was a trained rabbinical scholar of the highest order—or he could not have written Romans 5:12-21! Just think of how painstaking and detailed his writing could have been, but he always focused on the practical and inspirational. Let's do the same.

The Results of Our Justification (Romans 5:1-2)

> *5:1 Therefore, since we have been justified through faith, we have peace with God through our Lord Jesus Christ, 2 through whom we have gained access by faith into this grace in which we now stand. And we rejoice in the hope of the glory of God.*

The results of our justification are described here in a way that brings only positive feelings in putting our souls at rest. First, we have peace with God, which is a state of being, not simply a feeling (although we should certainly feel good about it!). The idea is that we are no longer enemies of God. Though we have all sinned and deserve to be separated from him, we are given peace with him through Christ. The larger subject of peace is developed

Biblically in some interesting ways, with some interpretative challenges. For example, according to Isaiah 9:6-7, Jesus was to be the Prince of Peace, bringing a never-ending increase of peace. Yet, he himself said, "Do not suppose that I have come to bring peace to the earth. I did not come to bring peace, but a sword" (Matthew 10:34). In John 16:33, he brought the two concepts together with these words: "I have told you these things, so that in me you may have peace. In this world you will have trouble." Therefore, in the spiritual realm, we can expect peace, but not in the physical realm.

Peace for disciples begins with our relationship with God and then leads to peace between brothers and sisters in God's kingdom. Thankfully, the cross has the power not only to bring us to God but to break down all racial hostilities, as we are told in Ephesians 2:14: "For he himself is our peace, who has made the two one and has destroyed the barrier, the dividing wall of hostility." As peacemakers (Matthew 5:9), we are to strive for peace with everyone, including those who persecute us (Romans 12:18-21). When we have these types of peace, surely "the peace of God, which transcends all understanding, will guard [our] hearts and [our] minds in Christ Jesus" (Philippians 4:7).

The second result of our justification in Romans 5 is that we stand in grace, which suggests the confidence and certainty we should have. Grace initially makes our justification possible, but then our justification means that we now stand in grace, and live daily in the state of grace. Grace does not just forgive; it makes us strong (2 Timothy 2:1), enabling us to stand firm against the devil's onslaughts. Only because of grace can we stand.

The third result of our justification here in Romans 5:2 is hope. Because we are no longer alienated from God and are confident that he is for us (Romans 8:31), we can face the future with hope. Biblically, hope is a combination of desire plus expectation, rather than simply wishful thinking. Note the connection between hope, love and the Holy Spirit a few verses later. Without God's grace, we could never have peace, strength or hope.

The Growth Through Our Justification (Romans 5:3-5)

> ³Not only so, but we also rejoice in our sufferings,
> because we know that suffering produces perseverance;

⁴perseverance, character; and character, hope. ⁵And hope
does not disappoint us, because God has poured out his love
into our hearts by the Holy Spirit, whom he has given us.

Growth never comes easily, for just as physical muscles are developed through struggle, so are spiritual "muscles." Notice the progression of this spiritual growth: Suffering is the first stage. Perseverance must follow (no wimping out!). Character is built as a result of the continuing struggle. Hope is the final stage. People who have persevered through the hard times can look at the future full of hope—they see what God has already done in their lives and they know that they are not quitters! Compare the progression mentioned in James 1:2-4. Trials come to test our faith. Perseverance through these trials is the second stage. Maturity is the result of keeping on keeping on when the going gets tough.

Next, compare the progression in Hebrews 12:4-15. Struggles and hardships are the starting place, here called "discipline" from God. Perseverance is implied ("later on" in v11). Righteousness and peace are produced as we share in God's holiness. Note the sobering truth that God's discipline can disable us (through discouragement) and/or make us bitter (vv13, 15)—if we react to it without faith that God is in control. Finally, compare these passages to the suffering of Jesus in Hebrews 5:7-10. Suffering was common in his life on the earth. Perseverance through the suffering is shown by his "loud cries" and "submission." Finally, he was perfected for his ministry as our high priest.

The same, exact progression is seen in all of these passages, giving us ample proof that we cannot grow otherwise! Being Christlike will never be easy, and it will never be quickly accomplished. But Jesus clearly warned us to "count the cost" before signing on with his movement (Luke 14:25-33). Once we have verbally confessed him as *Lord*, we had better follow through with our lives—for the rest of our lives!

The Basis of Our Justification (Romans 5:6-11)

⁶You see, at just the right time, when we were still
powerless, Christ died for the ungodly. ⁷Very rarely will
anyone die for a righteous man, though for a good man
someone might possibly dare to die. ⁸But God demonstrates

*his own love for us in this: While we were still sinners,
Christ died for us.*

*⁹Since we have now been justified by his blood, how
much more shall we be saved from God's wrath through
him! ¹⁰For if, when we were God's enemies, we were reconciled to him through the death of his Son, how much more,
having been reconciled, shall we be saved through his life!
¹¹Not only is this so, but we also rejoice in God through our
Lord Jesus Christ, through whom we have now received
reconciliation.*

Having talked about the results of justification, Paul returns
again to the basis of our justification in verses 6-11. It is obvious
that he does not want us to miss the point. That basis is, in
essence, the death of Jesus for the ungodly. Paul says that we
would not die for simply a righteous person. From the context, it
is clear that "righteous" is used here in the sense of being a person
who is decent though not outstanding. However, we might possibly die for a good person. (In the New Testament, the word "good"
is used in a very exalted but sparing manner.) How different is this
Jesus who died not for the decent or for the good, but for his
ungodly, powerless, sinful enemies—that's us, folks! Jesus' life
was given for those who have been reconciled. Having been reconciled—brought back to terms of friendship—by his death, we
are continually saved by his life. He is now our older brother, our
friend and our great high priest who longs to bless us (Hebrews
2:14-18, 4:14-16). Praise God for his grace!

A popular hymn speaks of our loving to tell the old, old story
of Jesus and his love. The challenge of doing this comes from the
fact that old stories can lose their luster, and the story of the cross
is no exception. I remember going to a gathering of Christians
some years back, and seeing a brother just sitting in his van for
quite a while, making no attempt to come in to the meeting. I went
up to the window of his vehicle and asked if he was okay. He said,
"Yes, but I just taught the cross study to someone, and it left me
with a lot of emotions." I felt envious as he said that, for keeping
a soft heart toward the cross is not always easy for me. Perhaps
the following story of unknown origin will help all of us *feel* the
message of the cross once again.

A Parable: The Substitution of Punishment

Once in the early days of America, a very poignant situation unfolded in the setting of a one-room schoolhouse. On a very consistent basis, one of the students was stealing from the other children's lunches in the mornings as they were stored in the cloakroom. Finally, the other students were so irate that they demanded a meeting with the teacher about the continuing problem of having their lunches pilfered. After some heated discussion, the students requested that the punishment for the thief, when caught, be twenty very hard "licks" from the teacher's "board of education" (a large wooden paddle with small holes drilled in it)!

Several weeks later, the teacher came back into the schoolhouse to get his sweater during the morning recess. Hearing a slight noise inside, he quietly entered the building and went into the cloakroom. There he found the thief, little Johnny, taking food from another child's lunchbox. This frail child was one of the youngest children in the school, about seven years old. As he began to cry, the teacher questioned about his stealing.

He sobbed out a very sad story. His father had died about nine months before, leaving behind a widow and five small children, the oldest of which was Johnny. He told of how destitute they were, and how the small amount of food they did have went to the younger children. He said that he was starving, and as the teacher looked more closely at his little body, he knew that it was true. But, the boy was still a thief and had to be brought before the other students for his punishment.

Johnny was crying and trembling as the other students listened to the teacher's account of how he had discovered the thief. As he then prepared to administer the punishment, a student in the back of the room spoke up. It turned out that this student, Bob, was the oldest boy in the school at age sixteen. He also happened to be the one whose lunch had been stolen on that particular day. "Teacher," he said, "I realize that we all agreed on twenty hard licks from your paddle. But did we say who had to take the licks?"

The teacher said, "Well, actually no, but I think we all assumed that the thief would take the punishment."

The older student replied, "Since we did not state exactly who had to be beaten, I want to stand in little Johnny's place and take his licks." With a large lump in his throat, the teacher nodded and motioned for the boy to come forward. As was the custom, the boy put his hands on the teacher's desk and bent over, facing the class. The teacher then hit him in the appropriate place as hard as he could twenty times.

By the time it was over, the teacher was crying, the students were crying, and little Johnny was crying most of all. No one present ever forgot the events of that day. Johnny never stole again, and his best friend for life became Bob, the one who took the punishment due him. Their relationship was such that they were like brothers for the rest of their lives.

This simple story illustrates just a bit of what took place on the cross of Jesus. As the song puts it, "I owed a debt I could not pay; he paid a debt he did not owe." Like Johnny, we should be motivated to give up our lives of sin and to love our Jesus with a never-ending appreciation!

Many Christians struggle with continued feelings of worthlessness, because they know all too well what they were like before becoming Christians, and they are quite aware of their sins as Christians. However, their problem is that they neither understand grace nor understand that their value is based on their nature rather than on their performance. Perhaps the following little illustration will help.

How Much Are You Really Worth?

An ugly bilious green chair sat on top of a trash pile awaiting the arrival of the garbage truck. Those who passed by and saw the chair thought to themselves, "I don't blame those people for throwing that hideous chair away. In fact, I wonder why it took them so long!"

However, one person had an entirely different reaction when he passed by and saw the chair. He quickly pulled his station wagon over to the curb, jumped out and grabbed the chair, put it in the back of his vehicle and drove away. When this antique dealer got the chair home, he began stripping off the many coats of paint until he was down to the original wood. Once restored, this chair was a thing of beauty and value! To the eyes of the unaware, the chair was junk, but to the trained eye of the antique dealer, it was an object to be esteemed. The layers of ugly paint did not take away the basic nature of the chair underneath it all.

Similarly, we have "painted" our lives with many ugly coats of sin, but the real value remains underneath the surface. Once the blood of Christ removes these hideous layers, our true natures may be seen once more. But what is it about our natures that gives us value in the first place? It is that we are made in the image of God himself (Genesis 1:27). We have the capability to reason, to feel, to appreciate, to love. And we have the capacity to live for eternity!

But how can we be sure that we are that valuable? Our value has been permanently established by the price God paid for us— his becoming a man and dying on the cross in our place. For a shirt, we would be willing to pay twenty or thirty dollars, and maybe more, depending on our financial situation and the quality of the shirt. But no one would pay a million dollars for it. The price we are willing to pay for something reflects its value to us. When God paid his unbelievable price for our souls, he set our value far beyond man's ability to comprehend. One little boy, whose theology far surpassed his grammar, said it this way: "God made me, and God don't make no junk." Let's believe that. Then let's live like we believe that!

The Power That Brought Justification (Romans 5:12-21)

> [12]*Therefore, just as sin entered the world through one man, and death through sin, and in this way death came to all men, because all sinned—*[13]*for before the law was given, sin was in the world. But sin is not taken into account when there is no law.* [14]*Nevertheless, death reigned from the time of Adam to the time of Moses, even over those who did not sin by breaking a command, as did Adam, who was a pattern of the one to come.*
> [15]*But the gift is not like the trespass. For if the many died by the trespass of the one man, how much more did God's grace and the gift that came by the grace of the one*

man, Jesus Christ, overflow to the many! [16]*Again, the gift of God is not like the result of the one man's sin: The judgment followed one sin and brought condemnation, but the gift followed many trespasses and brought justification.* [17]*For if, by the trespass of the one man, death reigned through that one man, how much more will those who receive God's abundant provision of grace and of the gift of righteousness reign in life through the one man, Jesus Christ.*

[18]*Consequently, just as the result of one trespass was condemnation for all men, so also the result of one act of righteousness was justification that brings life for all men.* [19]*For just as through the disobedience of the one man the many were made sinners, so also through the obedience of the one man the many will be made righteous.*

[20]*The law was added so that the trespass might increase. But where sin increased, grace increased all the more,* [21]*so that, just as sin reigned in death, so also grace might reign through righteousness to bring eternal life through Jesus Christ our Lord.*

By anyone's admission, this passage is one of the most difficult in the entire New Testament. In the case of difficult or obscure texts, the basic rule of interpretation is to not base a highly consequential doctrine on them, but rather look to other, clearer passages. Under no circumstances should a doctrine based on a difficult passage be allowed to contradict easily understood passages. We may not be absolutely sure of the exact meaning of a text, but when compared to other less difficult texts, we can usually be sure of what it does *not* mean. In the case of Romans 5, these basic principles must be kept firmly in mind as we offer an interpretation.

Three primary interpretations of Romans 5 can be found in the writings and teachings of different religious groups. The first would be the concept of original sin, as taught by the Catholic Church and a number of other churches as well. The doctrine claims that everyone is born guilty of the sin of Adam, and therefore everyone enters the world in a state of spiritual death. Infant baptism is then seen as a remedy to this condition. The second concept might be called the original choice concept. This explanation argues that

Adam introduced sin and Jesus introduced righteousness, &
now we can choose which path that we want to follow. In a sense,
this is obviously true, but it does not fit well with the actual
wording of Romans 5.

The view that I believe squares with both this passage and
with others all through the Bible is one that we might call the original consequence view. The idea is that Adam introduced sin, which
resulted in physical death for him. He was shut out of the Garden
of Eden, where the tree of life was located (Genesis 3:22-24). He
had been told in Genesis 2:16-17 that if he ate of the tree of the
knowledge of good and evil, he would surely die. This death penalty
would have had to indicate or include physical death, because of
the result that his sin brought. However, sin also separates man
from God spiritually, and at the point of his sin, Adam experienced
spiritual death as well. The "law of sin and death" in Romans 8:2
and passages like Isaiah 59:1-2 refer to this principle.

Adam's disobedience resulted in both types of death for him,
and it certainly resulted in physical death for all of his descendants, since they (we) were also barred from the tree of life.
Therefore, his sin did affect us physically, as far as the *consequences* are concerned. But did his sin affect us spiritually in a
way that makes us guilty of his sin? Herein lies the real issue. Two
passages in the Old Testament are quite helpful on this point. In
Exodus 20:5, God forbids idol worship with these words:

> *"You shall not bow down to them or worship them; for I,
> the LORD your God, am a jealous God, punishing the chil-
> dren for the sin of the fathers to the third and fourth gen-
> eration of those who hate me."*

Clearly, the consequences of our parents' sins, be they idolatry or
drunkenness, do hurt their families. But we are considering consequences, not actual guilt for another's actions. Ezekiel 18:20
dispels the whole theory of inherited guilt.

> *"The soul who sins is the one who will die. The son will not
> share the guilt of the father, nor will the father share the
> guilt of the son. The righteousness of the righteous man
> will be credited to him, and the wickedness of the wicked
> will be charged against him."*

In 1 John 3:4, John says, "Everyone who sins breaks the law." Sin is a personal action for which only the sinner is responsible. Guilt cannot be passed on, but consequences can. For example, if the president of the United States made decisions that brought the country into a war, we would not be responsible for his decision (excepting his advisory staff). We would, however, suffer the consequences. Therefore, because of Adam's first sin, we die physically, but we die spiritually because of our own sins. Let's go back to Romans 5 and see if this explanation harmonizes with the teaching of this passage.

The early part of the chapter showed the efficacious nature of Christ's death for mankind. Paul's Jewish opponents, whether in or out of the church, were apparently arguing that Christ's death could not possibly affect every person in the entire world, as Paul preached. They felt that his emphasis on the work of Christ was far overstated and would discourage the personal responsibility of individuals. He countered by showing that even Adam had affected everyone by sinning and being shut out of the Garden. Thus, we sinned in Adam in the sense that we share in the consequence of his actions.

The same basic analogy is found in 1 Corinthians 15:21-22 regarding the effects of Adam and Christ on all mankind: "For since death came through a man, the resurrection of the dead comes also through a man. For as in Adam all die, so in Christ all will be made alive." Compare this concept to a similar one in Hebrews 7:9-10, in which the Levitical priests are said to have paid tithes in a representative manner through their ancestor Abraham when he paid tithes to Melchizedek:

> One might even say that Levi, who collects the tenth, paid the tenth through Abraham, because when Melchizedek met Abraham, Levi was still in the body of his ancestor.

It should be clear that the New Testament traces consequences back to our ancestors, but this is quite different from tracing our guilt or responsibility back to their actions.

Much of Romans 5:12-21 discusses this type of *involuntary participation* on our part, in which we had absolutely no choice in the matter. Paul begins by showing that we die physically because of Adam's sin. An interpretative paraphrase of verses 13-14 would go something like this:

> Before the Mosaic law was given, sin was in the world, but sin did not demand the death penalty where there was no such law stating it (as was the case before the law, especially prior to the Flood). However, physical death still reigned between Adam and Moses, even over those who did not have the command "sin and die," as did Adam. Therefore, the people in this period *must* have died because of Adam's sin rather than their own sins.

Verses 15-17 form a parenthetical explanation of how Jesus' impact on humanity is far *greater* than that of Adam. The "gift" (v16), the "much more" (v17), and "God's abundant provision of grace" (v17) refer to spiritual salvation, which must be personally accepted. The basic thread of Paul's earlier argument—that we are raised from the dead because of the death and resurrection of Christ—continues in verses 18-19. The "life" and being "made righteous" refer to being raised bodily, good and evil alike. The term "righteous" is used in the sense of having the scales balanced out and earlier consequences offset. (The term does not always mean *spiritually* righteous, as Romans 5:7 demonstrates.) In John 5:28-29 Jesus states:

> *"Do not be amazed at this, for a time is coming when all who are in their graves will hear his voice and come out— those who have done good will rise to live, and those who have done evil will rise to be condemned."*

Paul concludes in a similar manner (vv20-21) as verses 15-17, showing the possibility of *voluntary participation* in the benefits of Christ's death. The "increased" sin refers to our sins, which bring spiritual death but can be forgiven. Therefore, both Adam and Christ affected everyone. What we lost in Adam (life in a body), we gain back in Christ at the resurrection. However, Christ affected everyone potentially much more by offering spiritual life.

The end result of Paul's line of reasoning is that he was not overstating the impact of Christ's work in man's behalf, and in the next chapter, he continues in a similar mode by dealing with the false charge that grace leads to a light view of sin (Romans 6:1-4). If the Jews could accept the universal impact brought about by Adam's sin, then they should have been able to apply the principle to Jesus and his work. Especially was this a feasible idea when the factor of Christ's *deity* was added to the formula!

Romans 5:12-21 is admittedly a very difficult chapter, but it cannot be interpreted in a way that causes it to contradict other clear passages. The interpretation provided here does seem to take these other passages into consideration, while attempting to deal honestly with the Romans text as well. To sum up this explanation, I will include my interpretative paraphrase of the passage.

> [12]*Therefore, just as sin entered the world through one man* (Adam) *and* (physical) *death through sin, and in this way* (physical) *death came to all men, because all sinned* (representatively in Adam, as far as the consequences were concerned)—[13]*for before the law* (of Moses) *was given, sin was in the world. But sin is not taken into account* (counted for the death penalty) *when there is no law* (demanding such a penalty). [14]*Nevertheless,* (physical) *death reigned from the time of Adam to the time of Moses, even over those who did not sin by breaking a command* (which carried the death penalty), *as did Adam, who was a pattern of the one* (Christ) *who was to come.*
>
> [15]*But* (before we go on discussing the impact of Adam on the world, and how Christ offset that impact, let us understand that) *the gift* (of Christ's impact on the world) *is not like the trespass* (it is far greater!). *For if the many* (everyone) *died* (physically) *by the trespass of the one man* (Adam), *how much more did God's grace and the gift that came by the grace of the one man, Jesus Christ, overflow to the many* (everyone)! [16]*Again, the gift of God is not like* (not limited to) *the result of the one man's sin: The judgment* (consequences) *followed one sin and brought* (physical) *condemnation, but the gift followed many* (Adam's and our own) *trespasses and brought* (the possibility of spiritual) *justification.* [17]*For if, by the trespass of the one man,* (physical) *death reigned through that one man, how much more will those who receive* (by personal response) *God's abundant provision*

of grace and of the gift of righteousness reign in life through the one man, Jesus Christ.

[18](But let's return to our discussion of the impact of Adam's sin and how Christ's resurrection offset that impact.) *Consequently, just as the result of one trespass was* (physical) *condemnation for all men, so also the result of one act of righteousness* (Jesus' resurrection after a sinless life) *was justification* (from the death sentence) *that brings life* (in a body at the resurrection at the Last Day) *for all men.* [19]*For just as through the disobedience of the one man the many* (everyone) *were made* sinners (as far as the consequences are concerned), *so also through the obedience of the one man the many* (everyone) *will be made righteous* (from the death penalty, because they will be raised from the dead).

[20](Now let's end this comparison by going back to the earlier idea of how Christ's impact did far more than offset the impact of Adam's sin—it ushered in the opportunity for spiritual life to all who accept it.) *The law* (of Moses) *was added so that the trespass* (each man's personal sins) *might increase. But where sin increased, grace increased all the more,* [21]*so that, just as sin reigned in death* (physically because of Adam's sin and spiritually because of our own sins), *so also grace might reign through righteousness to bring* (to those who choose it) *eternal life through Jesus Christ our Lord.*

Even when this passage is shown to not teach the doctrine of original sin, other passages are incorrectly used to support the doctrine, especially Psalm 51:5: "Surely I was sinful at birth, sinful from the time my mother conceived me." David wrote this psalm after he had taken responsibility for his sin with Bathsheba and was quite broken and repentant. The last thing that he was trying to do was to shift the blame to his mother or anyone else. Contextually, original sin does not fit. David totally accepted responsibility by admitting that he had been born into a sinful world and had participated in its evil for as long as he could remember. To make that point as strongly as possible, he used a figure of speech called "hyperbole," in which a case is overstated for emphasis. Hyperbole is used in other psalms, such as Psalm 22:9, 58:3 and 71:6. The example in Psalm 58:3 is an excellent

...allel to Psalm 51, as it states: "Even from birth the wicked go astray; from the womb they are wayward and speak lies."

Another passage often used to attempt to substantiate this doctrine of original sin is Ephesians 2:1-3. In verse 3, it says that "we were by nature objects of wrath." The word "nature" may refer to inborn nature or it may refer to acquired nature. In this context, the latter seems obvious, because the emphasis is on what *we* have done—our personal sins and sinful lifestyles—certainly not on what *Adam* had done. The very idea that we could somehow inherit personal guilt for Adam's actions raises numerous questions. First, why was there never a provision granting forgiveness for original sin in any covenant of God with man? Not even the sacrificial laws of the Mosaic covenant, which covered all kinds of sins, ever mention this type of sin. Second, if our fallen natures (which supposedly came from Adam's sin) now cause us to sin, why did Adam sin? Actually, he had fewer temptations to deal with than we do at the time of his first sin. For example, he did not have a temptation to commit adultery or to steal. Yet, he was tempted and sinned, just as we do—and was no better and no worse than we are. Third, why did we inherit only his *first* sin?

Perhaps the biggest fallacy in the whole idea of inherited sin ties in with our basic nature and how we became human beings in the first place. We receive our physical bodies from our earthly parents through procreation. Thus, all that we can inherit from them are physical attributes, including personality tendencies. On the other hand, our spirits come directly from God, and only from God can we inherit spiritual attributes. In Zechariah 12:1, we read, "The LORD, who stretches out the heavens, who lays the foundation of the earth, and who forms the spirit of man within him...." Ecclesiastes 12:7 speaks of both our bodies and spirits in this manner: "and the dust returns to the ground it came from, and the spirit returns to God who gave it." Hebrews 12:9 similarly reads, "Moreover, we have all had human fathers who disciplined us and we respected them for it. How much more should we submit to the Father of our spirits and live!" Therefore, we cannot inherit sin from our earthly fathers, for our spiritual nature (including our souls) comes directly from our heavenly Father!

✠

As we conclude our study of Romans 5, let us not lose touch with the real message of this chapter. It is all about Jesus taking our place on the cross, pouring out his lifeblood for our sins. In the words of Paul in 2 Corinthians 5:21, "God made him who had no sin to be sin for us, so that in him we might become the righteousness of God." But what does this really mean? It means that on the cross, Jesus, the perfectly righteous One, was judged as unrighteous so that we, the unrighteous, might be judged as righteous. It means that on the cross, Jesus made up for all that you and I have failed to do and to be. It means that on the cross, God ordered sin to execution in the person of his own Son. It means that on the cross, God dealt with Jesus as he must deal with sin—in harsh and unrelenting terms—that we might be dealt with as though we had never sinned. I'm stupefied, staggered and smitten by what I see at Calvary, and hopefully surrendered at the foot of the cross. God deserves nothing less

6

Dead to Sin—Alive in Christ

Romans 6

In the previous chapter, we saw the possibility of our receiving God's much-needed grace. We also saw the staggering price tag placed on that grace—the death of Jesus on a cross. We owed a debt we could not pay; he paid a debt he did not owe. Obviously, the cross took care of our sin problem in one sense, but that does not mean that sin ceases to be an issue for us. In some ways, the battle has just begun when we make Jesus the Lord of our daily lives. Not only do we need to find forgiveness from sin; we need to die to it on a continual basis. This chapter shows us what death to sin really entails.

The Reality (Romans 6:1-7)

> *6:1 What shall we say, then? Shall we go on sinning so that grace may increase? 2By no means! We died to sin; how can we live in it any longer? 3Or don't you know that all of us who were baptized into Christ Jesus were baptized into his death? 4We were therefore buried with him through baptism into death in order that, just as Christ was raised from the dead through the glory of the Father, we too may live a new life.*
>
> *5If we have been united with him like this in his death, we will certainly also be united with him in his resurrection. 6For we know that our old self was crucified with him so that the body of sin might be done away with, that we should no longer be slaves to sin—7because anyone who has died has been freed from sin.*

Paul begins Romans 6 by addressing his critics, as mentioned also back in Romans 3:8. His opponents thought that his placing so much emphasis on grace and forgiveness would lighten people's view of sin. But the fact is that much forgiveness produces much love. Hear what Jesus said to the so-called "sinful woman" who anointed his feet with her tears and perfume: "Therefore, I tell you, her many sins have been forgiven—for she loved much. But he who has been forgiven little loves little" (Luke 7:47). Is it not ironic that Satan often convinces us of the exact opposite of the truth?

No one can take sin lightly if they love God. My earthly father was once a very strong man who put fear into me. I did what he said more from fear than from love when I was a boy. In my adult life, however, we developed a very close relationship as great friends. Before his death, he was old and feeble physically. Certainly I had no fear of him at that point. Yet, I would have done virtually anything that he asked of me and never wanted to hurt or fail him in any way. Why? Because of *love*! In our relationship with God, the godly fear should always be there to some degree, but the primary motivation should be love. No one who truly loves God with all his heart, soul, mind and strength would ever want to hurt him.

In Romans 6:2-7, Paul shows that death to sin occurs when we are baptized into the death of Christ.[1] Although Christ died for everyone (Hebrews 2:9), no one benefits from this death until he personally *participates* in it. (Compare Hebrews 2:9 with Hebrews 5:9.) Hence, God views baptism into Christ's death as our personal acceptance of the cross and our only hope of salvation. These verses help answer important questions about baptism (and keep in mind that there is but one baptism that is acceptable to God—Ephesians 4:5).

First, what is baptism? Biblically, it is a burial in water, a going down into the water, as may be seen when Philip baptized the Ethiopian (Acts 8:34-39). The word translated "baptism" (*baptizo* in the Greek) means "to overwhelm, to plunge, to immerse." In the best known translations of the Bible, this Greek word was never actually translated into English, but only anglicized and brought directly into our language. This approach avoided a translation that would be contrary to the practices of most religious groups and also avoided a direct mistranslation at the same time. This was most unfortunate. In a practical sense, dead people are not buried by sprinkling a little dirt on them. Neither are people buried in baptism by sprinkling a little water on them.

Second, who is a Biblical candidate for baptism? Someone old enough to respond in true Biblical faith. In all passages on baptism, it is always associated with faith and repentance. Never do we find an example of a baby being baptized in the New Testament. Babies do not need to be baptized to be *saved*, because they are already *safe* (for they are without sin). Note that Paul described himself as being alive spiritually as a child and then as later reaching the age of accountability, at which time his sins were counted against him, bringing about his spiritual death (Romans 7:9). Read Romans 7:7-12 carefully, and you will see that no other meaning of verse 9 makes sense in context.

Third, why are people to be baptized—what is its purpose? The purpose is to personally accept Christ's death as the only solution for our sins. (Be sure to see also Acts 2:38, 22:16; Galatians 3:26-27; Colossians 2:12; Titus 3:5; and 1 Peter 3:21.) It is a response of faith to the cross. Viewed in this way, baptism should never be called a "work." Those who dare call it such, and they are many, totally misunderstand the difference between the basis of forgiveness and a condition of forgiveness. The basis, or merit, of forgiveness is the blood of Jesus. A condition is anything God requires of us as a faith response. Imagine that I promised you $100,000 if you would simply go to a certain bank at 10:00 A.M. on a certain date, talk to the president of the bank, and request my check, already made out to you. After you followed those simple instructions and received the money, would you brag about your great "work" of "earning" $100,000 in the space of thirty minutes, or would you praise me for my grace? Obvious, right? This should be our response in baptism.

We trust the death of Jesus for salvation when we are baptized, not the act of baptism itself. The explanation in the introduction is worth repeating: Baptism is a condition of salvation, not the basis (meriting factor). We each felt totally saved after our baptism. But as time goes by, too many of us are unsure of our salvation. Just as baptism was that *original* condition, repentance and prayer are *continuing* conditions (Acts 8:22, 1 John 1:7-9). After you repent and pray, do you feel less cleansed than you did at baptism? If yes, then you are trusting the condition far too much and the Author of the condition far too little.

In baptism, we not only participate in the death of Christ, but also in his resurrection (vv4-5). This resurrection life is empowered by the Holy Spirit, as Paul further describes in Romans 8:11: "And if the Spirit of him who raised Jesus from the dead is living in you, he who raised Christ from the dead will also give life to your mortal bodies through his Spirit, who lives in you." Since it is our mortal bodies that are given life, Paul is obviously talking about the victorious Christian life and not the final resurrection.

The Conviction (Romans 6:8-14)

⁸Now if we died with Christ, we believe that we will also live with him. ⁹For we know that since Christ was raised from the dead, he cannot die again; death no longer has mastery over him. ¹⁰The death he died, he died to sin once for all; but the life he lives, he lives to God.

¹¹In the same way, count yourselves dead to sin but alive to God in Christ Jesus. ¹²Therefore do not let sin reign in your mortal body so that you obey its evil desires. ¹³Do not offer the parts of your body to sin, as instruments of wickedness, but rather offer yourselves to God, as those who have been brought from death to life; and offer the parts of your body to him as instruments of righteousness. ¹⁴For sin shall not be your master, because you are not under law, but under grace.

Our death to sin is to be as final as Christ's one death for sin (vv8-10). To any disciple who is drawn away from this conviction, Paul has this challenge: "count yourselves dead to sin" (v11). After baptism into Christ, there must be no back-door policy! Anytime one is tempted, he must say, "No, I died to that." Nothing less will enable us to change and stay changed for good. As you envision yourself being a certain way for the rest of your life, you are on the road to permanent change.

When I was a young man, I developed the detestable habit of smoking. I obviously was not too smart, but I was smart enough to know that my health was being adversely affected by inhaling poisonous gases. I tried to quit many times. In fact, I told people that quitting smoking was actually quite easy—I had done it dozens of times! My problem was that I always had a back door, the knowledge that I could go back to smoking if stopping seemed too hard to me. Only when I could envision myself never smoking for the rest of my life was I able to quit permanently, and it was far easier than I could have imagined. Making irrevocable decisions can accomplish wonders, which is why developing deep convictions about spiritual issues is so vital.

In Romans 6:12-13, we find how to keep our convictions in place: just *feed the right dog!* All of us have two natures inside—the spiritual nature and the worldly nature (see Galatians 5:15-25). Imagine that each nature is a dog of equal size. Which one will win as they battle each other? The one you feed the most! Your goal needs to be to starve your worldly nature, while feeding your spiritual nature through the Word, prayer and fellowship.

According to Romans 6:14, our death to sin is made possible because we are not under law, but under grace. We are not under law as a means of earning righteousness, for grace is our only solution. However, we *are* under law as a guide for our lives of faith in God, for in 1 Corinthians 9:20-21 Paul said specifically that he was "under Christ's law." The correct conviction (a grace orientation) about our salvation produces freedom from sin's power; the incorrect conviction (a works orientation) brings frustration and failure as sin masters us time and time again. We simply must get past our pasts. Continuing to have a guilt-trip approach and a burdened heart cannot glorify God nor free our consciences. Paul felt bad about his past, but not guilty about it. Therefore, he could share about it to motivate both himself (1 Corinthians 15:10) and others (1 Timothy 1:15-16). Whatever you have done, it probably does not compare to the heinousness of Paul's sin of persecuting the church, to the point of killing disciples. Regarding your past, be thankful for the good, repent of the bad, learn from both good and bad, and then move on as you trust

God's grace. Yesterday is history; tomorrow is a mystery; today is a gift from God, which is why it is called the "present"!

The Righteous Life (Romans 6:15-23)

> [15]*What then? Shall we sin because we are not under law but under grace? By no means!* [16]*Don't you know that when you offer yourselves to someone to obey him as slaves, you are slaves to the one whom you obey—whether you are slaves to sin, which leads to death, or to obedience, which leads to righteousness?* [17]*But thanks be to God that, though you used to be slaves to sin, you wholeheartedly obeyed the form of teaching to which you were entrusted.* [18]*You have been set free from sin and have become slaves to righteousness.*
>
> [19]*I put this in human terms because you are weak in your natural selves. Just as you used to offer the parts of your body in slavery to impurity and to ever-increasing wickedness, so now offer them in slavery to righteousness leading to holiness.* [20]*When you were slaves to sin, you were free from the control of righteousness.* [21]*What benefit did you reap at that time from the things you are now ashamed of? Those things result in death!* [22]*But now that you have been set free from sin and have become slaves to God, the benefit you reap leads to holiness, and the result is eternal life.* [23]*For the wages of sin is death, but the gift of God is eternal life in Christ Jesus our Lord.*

Even though disciples have died to sin, they face an ongoing choice to stay that way. Be aware that the ultimate issue is a question of slavery. Whose slave are you? (vv15-18). We have no choice of whether or not we will be slaves. The only choice is, who will be our master—God or Satan? Notice the progression in verses 17-18: *lost* (slaves to sin), *obeyed* a form (pattern) of teaching (from the heart), and *saved* (set free from sin). In context, this progression describes the process in the early part of the chapter: it takes place at the point of baptism.

Be warned that no one can stay the same! (vv19-23). Wickedness increases, or righteousness and holiness increase. Again, which "dog" are you feeding? In verse 21, Paul's comments bring to mind an important question for each of us: How do you view your sinful past? Some view their pasts too lightly—they joke about their sins and may even seem to miss committing them. This is Paul's point here. In general, it seems that one of Paul's main concerns in Romans 6 is to get Christians to see that they can become slaves of sin again if they are lax and don't make the continual choice to give themselves to righteousness.

✠

The final verse in Romans 6 encapsulates the message of the first six chapters: sin earns death, but God gives life. We whose wages should be death are freely pardoned through our Master's work at Golgotha. Instead of the separation of death that we deserve, we receive the gift of sweet fellowship with our Maker and Master, for time and for eternity. Through his abundant grace, we now have a life that is truly life (1 Timothy 6:19). "Thanks be to God for his indescribable gift!" (2 Corinthians 9:15)

Note

1. For more details regarding denominational teaching about baptism and about Biblical teaching on the subject, see chapter 8 in my book *Prepared to Answer* (Billerica, Mass.: Discipleship Publications International, 1998) 105-118.

7

Dead to Legalism
Romans 7

Romans 7, in further discussing our death to sin, addresses the freedom from legalism that it brings. Since the Jews had perverted the law into a legalistic system, Paul argues that we are dead to law in Christ. Again, he is not saying that God's word is not a law that must be obeyed, but rather that law, as it was popularly viewed and used, only condemns. Such a view makes salvation depend on our performance, our ability to measure up to God's standards. The psalmist, although under the law, understood this principle totally, as he wrote:

> If you, O LORD, kept a record of sins,
> O Lord, who could stand? (Psalm 130:3)

Those who go in the direction of legalism seem to instinctively realize that they cannot keep everything in the Scriptures perfectly, so they distill the commandments down to the ones they think are most important and worry little about the rest. In the religious Jews' case, they also added their own traditions into the mix. These they even exalted above Scripture, as men are always prone to do, since these traditions really define them. Strong denominational adherents will generally not mind differences in interpreting a given passage, but they will fight tooth and nail for the creedal positions that define their denomination.

And thus it was in the first century. The Jews had their system of determining which commands were deemed weighty and which were not, which helps explain why they had such a challenge trying to deal with Jesus. He constantly broke their favorite traditions, knowing how they were going to feel and react!

Any view that keeps people from dependence on, and gratitude for, the grace of God is heaven's enemy and the enemy of men's souls. Therefore, Paul will in this chapter deal the coup de grace to the meritorious view of salvation, for it stands in opposition to the true doctrine of faith justification.

Dead to Law—It Is *Official* (Romans 7:1-6)

> [7:1] *Do you not know, brothers—for I am speaking to men who know the law—that the law has authority over a man only as long as he lives?* [2] *For example, by law a married woman is bound to her husband as long as he is alive, but if her husband dies, she is released from the law of marriage.* [3] *So then, if she marries another man while her husband is still alive, she is called an adulteress. But if her husband dies, she is released from that law and is not an adulteress, even though she marries another man.*
>
> [4] *So, my brothers, you also died to the law through the body of Christ, that you might belong to another, to him who was raised from the dead, in order that we might bear fruit to God.* [5] *For when we were controlled by the sinful nature, the sinful passions aroused by the law were at work in our bodies, so that we bore fruit for death.* [6] *But now, by dying to what once bound us, we have been released from the law so that we serve in the new way of the Spirit, and not in the old way of the written code.*

The general law of marriage is used as an illustration, because marriage is intended for life, to be broken only by death (vv1-3). The spiritual application is that man's bond to law is broken by the death of Christ, making us then free to marry him (v4). The law in view here is primarily the Mosaic Law, although we are also delivered from the law *principle* of trying to legalistically earn our salvation by performance. Any law can be perverted into legalism, and although the Old Testament tended more toward that corruption than does the New Testament, church history is replete with examples of such NT corruption. Obviously, to those of Jewish background in Paul's audience, the application was to those holding onto the Law of Moses.

The result in our lives is that under law, we were controlled by the sinful nature, and we bore fruit for death; now under Christ, we serve him in the Spirit, for we are spiritually minded rather than legalistic (v6). The idea of being married to Christ is also taught clearly in 2 Corinthians 11:2 and Ephesians 5:31-32. Since we are married to Christ, we bear fruit to God, which includes the idea of reproducing spiritual babies through this union (v4).

Dead to Law—It Is *Essential* (Romans 7:7-13)

> [7]*What shall we say, then? Is the law sin? Certainly not! Indeed I would not have known what sin was except through the law. For I would not have known what coveting really was if the law had not said, "Do not covet."* [8]*But sin, seizing the opportunity afforded by the commandment, produced in me every kind of covetous desire. For apart from law, sin is dead.* [9]*Once I was alive apart from law; but when the commandment came, sin sprang to life and I died.* [10]*I found that the very commandment that was intended to bring life actually brought death.* [11]*For sin, seizing the opportunity afforded by the commandment, deceived me, and through the commandment put me to death.* [12]*So then, the law is holy, and the commandment is holy, righteous and good.*
> [13]*Did that which is good, then, become death to me? By no means! But in order that sin might be recognized as sin, it produced death in me through what was good, so that through the commandment sin might become utterly sinful.*

Our death to law does not mean that the law itself was bad. In fact, it had very important purposes.[1] It defined sin (v7) and increased sin (v8), thereby making us more aware of our need for forgiveness; and it revealed sin in our lives (v9). The word of God acts as a mirror of the soul, according to James 1:23-25. A mirror shows our imperfections, and in the case of the spiritual mirror, we are to be moved to stay humble before God. As mentioned previously, Romans 7:9 teaches that Paul was innocent at an early age ("alive apart from law") but at a later age, the law came into force in his life ("sin sprang to life"—God now held him accountable), and he died (was separated from God spiritually). Exactly when this age of accountability occurs varies from child to child, but it may well be around the time of puberty, since sexual desires are such a part of the human struggle.

In verses 11-12, Paul concludes that the law is good. It contains God-breathed oracles, so how could it be bad? Law, as designed, made man dependent on God; law, as perverted, made man dependent on self, thereby removing the grace of God from the law. Law with God can cause an inspired person to exclaim "Oh, how I love your law!" (Psalm 119:97), but law without God damns the soul. We all must constantly guard against viewing and using law—any law—as an end within itself, for slipping into legalism is about as easy to do as to breathe. Satan sees to that.

Dead to Law—It Is *Paradoxical* (Romans 7:14-25)

> [14]We know that the law is spiritual; but I am unspiritual, sold as a slave to sin. [15]I do not understand what I do. For what I want to do I do not do, but what I hate I do. [16]And if I do what I do not want to do, I agree that the law is good. [17]As it is, it is no longer I myself who do it, but it is sin living in me. [18]I know that nothing good lives in me, that is, in my sinful nature. For I have the desire to do what is good, but I cannot carry it out. [19]For what I do is not the good I want to do; no, the evil I do not want to do—this I keep on doing. [20]Now if I do what I do not want to do, it is no longer I who do it, but it is sin living in me that does it.
>
> [21]So I find this law at work: When I want to do good, evil is right there with me. [22]For in my inner being I delight in God's law; [23]but I see another law at work in the members of my body, waging war against the law of my mind and making me a prisoner of the law of sin at work within my members. [24]What a wretched man I am! Who will rescue me from this body of death? [25]Thanks be to God—through Jesus Christ our Lord!
>
> So then, I myself in my mind am a slave to God's law, but in the sinful nature a slave to the law of sin.

To really understand the law and the condemnation it wrought in our lives, we must understand its paradoxical nature (vv14-25). The paradoxes are difficult to deal with on a consistent basis, especially on an emotional level. For example, we are not under law (Romans 6:14), yet we are under law (1 Corinthians 9:21). We are not saved *by* works (Ephesians 2:8-9), yet we are not saved *without* works (James 2:14-26). We must obey with all of our hearts, yet our obedience does not merit righteousness. We cannot work to earn our salvation, yet we must work out our salvation with fear and trembling! (Philippians 2:12).

Obviously, the line between correct and incorrect understanding can seem to be a fine one indeed. When we live with the correct understanding, life is fulfilling; when we live with the incorrect one, life is frustrating. Romans 7:14-25 graphically describes the latter situation. Much ink has been used discussing who Paul must have been describing in this passage. Some say it describes Paul as a Christian, while others say it describes Paul as a Jew. A variation of the second view claims that Paul used the first person in the present tense to be more graphic in showing his frustration as a Pharisee and of any person who seeks law justification. This view seems to square with the text and other texts the best.

On the surface, Paul was likely not in touch with the amount of his inner turmoil until grace found his heart. In Philippians 3:6, he wrote that he was "faultless" in legalistic righteousness. Addressing the Sanhedrin in Jerusalem, he claimed to have lived before God in all good conscience (Acts 23:1). Surely Paul was one of the most exemplary Jewish leaders in all of Israel. But I have to wonder just why he was so filled with rage at Christians. A good amount of frustration and inner turmoil seems to be the most likely answer. After all, this phenomenon is not uncommon, for we all learn to stuff inner pain when we do not believe that solutions exist.

On the practical level, all of us experience the feelings expressed in this passage at various times, for all of us slip into a legalistic mind-set. This is why the passage is written at this point of Paul's argument—he drives home the truth of how useless a performance orientation actually is! God does not want any of us to feel such frustration and failure. Being guilt ridden does not bring God glory, and it does nothing to produce in us real spirituality. In fact, living with a Romans 7 conscience is about the poorest advertisement for Christianity that we could possibly find.

Certainly this passage was not intended to be descriptive of the disciple's normal life, although it can seem to be. Note the following Biblical principles that demonstrate God's plan for our spiritual victory over the misery depicted in Romans 7:

1. We are under bondage to Christ, not to sin (Romans 6:16).

2. We sin, but we do not *practice* sin (1 John 3:7-9).

3. Christ, not sin, dwells in us (Galatians 2:20).

4. We can follow through in faithful obedience with God's power (1 Corinthians 10:13; Philippians 2:12-13, 4:13).

5. Although there is a struggle between flesh and spirit (Galatians 5:17), the Spirit *wins* in a demonstrable way, for by his power, our lives can be worthy of imitation (1 Corinthians 4:16-17, 11:1; Philippians 3:15-17, 4:9; 1 Thessalonians 2:10-12).

6. The law of the Spirit frees us from the law of sin and death (Romans 8:2).

7. We are filled with rejoicing (Philippians 4:4, 1 Thessalonians 5:16), not with the frustration and failure that is described in Romans 7!

Too many of us do live in Romans 7 and need desperately to move on to life in Romans 8. The most important ingredient in making that transition is how we see God and how we think he sees us. Prayerfully, the following illustrations will help you to see God in a way that indeed frees you up to serve in the newness of the Spirit and not the oldness of the letter.

What Kind of Father Do You Think He Is?

A little boy forgot to feed his dog one night. The next morning, his dad asked if he had fed his dog the night before, and then gave him the appropriate correction, telling him not to forget again. The boy apologized to his father for the earlier mistake every night, and his father kept assuring him that he was forgiven and had obviously learned his lesson. But the apologizing continued, and at some point the forgiving dad eventually said, "What kind of a father do you think I am, anyway?" Not accepting forgiveness shows a lack of trust in God's nature. What kind of Father do you think God is, anyway?

What Does He Really Want from Us?

Our world is so immersed in a performance orientation that it is difficult to conceive of anything else. Even our families often tied their acceptance of us to our performance. We are conditioned to feel good when we perform well and feel bad when we do not, which is understandable. But this condition often translates to us as disciples as feeling saved when we perform well and lost when we do not. Obviously, I feel bad when my relationship with my wife goes awry, but I do not feel *unmarried*!

When you think of serving God, how do you picture the two of you? Many picture God as the Master and themselves as servants. This, of course, is a Biblical analogy, but it does not nearly provide the whole scenario of our relationship with him. In fact, if that is our primary conception of the relationship, we will often feel more duty than desire in our service.

As mentioned earlier, Christians are married to Christ (Romans 7:4, 2 Corinthians 11:2, Ephesians 5:31-32). As a happily married husband of thirty-six years, I think I have a fair grasp on what that analogy is designed to teach. When I arise in the mornings, I don't start thinking, "I hope Theresa does all the things for me that I think she should for a change," and then mentally start going down some checklist of her duties. I just want to see her, to be with her, to talk with her. She is my delight, and as the song by Joshua Kadison says, she "will always be beautiful in my eyes." I am not thinking about her serving me; I'm thinking about her loving me. Of course, because she does love me (amazing, isn't it?) she will do many things to serve me, and I her, but neither of us is focused on the doing. We are focused on the *being*—being in love! Do you think Jesus is a different kind of husband than I am? Frankly, he is much more focused on serving you than on you serving him.

Probably the most used Biblical analogy portraying our relationship with God is that of a Father with his children. Again, since I have two grown children whom I love dearly (along with their awesome mates), I understand the analogy. When I go to visit them, I am not thinking of all that they ought to do for me. I am much more focused on what I want to do for them because I love them so much. I just want to see them, to be with them, to laugh and to love. Now, in the course of our time together, they will do many things to serve me, for we love each other deeply. But the emphasis is never on the doing; it is on the being. They do not sit around wondering if they measure up to my expectations, for they do not have to earn my approval. They already have it—in spades! Do you see the point? When you are in love, duty becomes desire. That is how God feels about serving you. Is that how you feel about serving him?

The power of our serving must be in the relationship, not in the tasks themselves. He is mostly concerned about us knowing and loving him, according to Jesus in John 17:3: "'Now this is eternal life: that they may know you, the only true God, and Jesus Christ, whom you have sent.'" If we have this kind of relationship, the serving will be a joy. Now that is good news. But it gets even better. He provides the power to do the serving that he calls us to do. In fact, he does in us and through us what we could never do ourselves. As Paul put it in Galatians 2:20,

> I have been crucified with Christ and I no longer live, but Christ lives in me. The life I live in the body, I live by faith in the Son of God, who loved me and gave himself for me.

Here he contrasts the life focused on relationship in Christ with a life focused on performance. The former he calls a life of faith, a life empowered by God though the cross. Note that the "self-life" is crucified (and not just our *sins*), making available Christ's life in us. No wonder Paul could say "when I am weak, then I am strong" (2 Corinthians 12:10). His work ethic was staggering, but only because he had learned the difference between working in God's power and his own.

> But by the grace of God I am what I am, and his grace to me was not without effect. No, I worked harder than all of them—yet not I, but the grace of God that was with me. (1 Corinthians 15:10)

Men are full of glib sayings, such as "If it is to be, it is up to me," and "God helps those who help themselves." You stay on that track and you will end up in Romans 7 before long. We entered a relationship with Christ simply by trusting his blood as we were lowered beneath the waters of baptism. We maintain that relationship by that same trust, the surrendered faith that really believes that he must be the power in us to accomplish his will in us. That is why he gives us the Holy Spirit when we are baptized (Acts 2:38). We can allow our humanistic tendencies to take us far afield, and to inflate us with far too much self-importance. It may sound somehow noble to say "God has no hands but our hands and no feet but our feet," but he is much bigger than that. God doesn't need you, for as Acts 17:25 says, "He is not served by human hands, as if he needed anything, because he himself gives all men life and breath and everything else." No, he doesn't *need* you; but, amazingly, he *wants* you. And that is the marvel of it all!

Don't you think it is about time to relax and enjoy the love God longs to lavish on you, and then out of that relationship allow his power in you to draw others to him? It is a faith walk with him, not simply a belief that he exists and wrote the Bible and will one day judge us all by it. Our faith is forever totally centered in him, "that out of his glorious riches he may strengthen you with power through his Spirit in your inner being, so that Christ may dwell in your hearts through faith" (Ephesians 3:16-17).[2]

✝

The final two verses of Romans 7 are pivotal indeed, as verse 24 captures the utter misery produced by legalism and the first part of verse 25 shows the release grace offers our tormented souls. The latter fits into the theme of Romans 8, but Paul couldn't wait to get there, it would seem. He had to shout, in essence, "Hallelujah!"

Our struggle to be righteous by performing has one good side: it brings us to the poverty of spirit described in Matthew 5:3 when we see that we cannot pull ourselves up spiritually by our own boot straps. Then and only then will we say, "Thanks be to God, I can be saved through Jesus Christ! Amen!"

Notes

1. For more detail about these purposes, see appendix 1, "Purposes of the Mosaic Law."

2. Most of this last section is taken from my book *The Victory of Surrender—Second Edition* (Billerica, Mass.: Discipleship Publications International, 1999), 196-200.

8

Free at Last!
Romans 8

Romans 8 reveals the complete release and relief that the prior seven chapters have pointed to. Put simply, there is now no condemnation for those who are in a relationship with Christ. God has given us everything we need to enter that relationship and to live in that relationship of grace for our entire lives. Therefore, while it is possible to fall from grace, it is totally unnecessary—grace is big enough to provide everything we need to keep us right with God. In one sense the term "fallaway" is not accurate—those who leave God are "walkaways" who deliberately walk away from the outstretched hands of Jesus and the pleading voice of God!

Delivered from the Law of Sin and Death (Romans 8:1-8)

8:1 Therefore, there is now no condemnation for those who are in Christ Jesus, ²because through Christ Jesus the law of the Spirit of life set me free from the law of sin and death. ³For what the law was powerless to do in that it was weakened by the sinful nature, God did by sending his own Son in the likeness of sinful man to be a sin offering. And so he condemned sin in sinful man, ⁴in order that the righteous requirements of the law might be fully met in us, who do not live according to the sinful nature but according to the Spirit.

⁵Those who live according to the sinful nature have their minds set on what that nature desires; but those who live in accordance with the Spirit have their minds set on what the Spirit desires. ⁶The mind of sinful man is death, but the mind controlled by the Spirit is life and peace; ⁷the sinful mind is hostile to God. It does not submit to God's law, nor can it do so. ⁸Those controlled by the sinful nature cannot please God.

Paul begins with a thrilling assertion: *No condemnation in Christ!* Just what in Romans 8 proves this wonderful point? In Christ, we have been delivered from the law of sin and death. What does it mean to be "in Christ"? It means that we are in a relationship with him. Only three NT passages say specifically how we enter (into) that precious relationship, and all say that we are baptized into it: Romans 6:3-4, Galatians 3:26-27, and 1 Corinthians 12:13. We maintain it by walking faithfully in the light of God's word (1 John 1:5-10). We lose it only by being unrepentant toward our sin, thus allowing sin to become full-grown in our hearts and lives (James 1:13-15).

What is the law of "sin and death"? It is that law which Adam and Eve were originally under, where one sin put them out of fellowship with God. (Later, of course, he provided grace for them as well.) It is the principle that operates in the life of every person out of Christ, which means that every sin of every type is entered on their record before God. It is law without grace, demand without deliverance, obligation without the power to perform. It is the position of lostness, out of which God desperately wants to deliver everyone!

What can set us free from the law of sin and death? Not the Law of Moses, says Paul (v3). The Law of Moses was powerless to free man from his sin problem. Once a violation of law occurs, that law has no power to forgive the violation—it simply identifies the violation. However, the law of the Spirit of life (v2), which is to say the gospel of Christ, can set us free. Additionally, by the power of the Spirit, we are now able to live the righteous life that God calls us to live (v4). Having been freed from the law or principle of performance, we are now under the law or principle of grace. This new freedom enables us to perform much better now that we do not sense a guillotine hanging over our necks. As 1 Corinthians 15:56-57 puts it, "The sting of death is sin, and the power of sin is the law. But thanks be to God! He gives us the victory through our Lord Jesus Christ."

Paul describes here two ways that people can live. They can live according to the flesh, that is the sinful nature (*kata sarx*), or they live according to the Spirit (*kata pneuma*). To live *kata sarx* is to live depending on yourself, and the result of that is spiritual death (v13). But to live *kata pneuma* is to live depending on the Spirit and the result of that is life and peace (v6). If as disciples we begin to live *kata sarx* again, we are feeding the wrong dog and in grave danger of losing what we have found.

What can keep us living in the Spirit? A spiritual mind-set is the answer, and whatever we dwell on in our minds will work its way into our hearts (vv5-8). Colossians 3:1-2 tells us to set both our hearts (emotions) and our minds on things above. Whatever is in our heart will occupy our minds, but whatever we deliberately put into our minds will work down into our hearts. It is a choice and a decision to develop spiritual character. Let's do it!

The Holy Spirit (Romans 8:9-17)

⁹You, however, are controlled not by the sinful nature but by the Spirit, if the Spirit of God lives in you. And if anyone does not have the Spirit of Christ, he does not belong to Christ. ¹⁰But if Christ is in you, your body is dead because of sin, yet your spirit is alive because of righteousness. ¹¹And if the Spirit of him who raised Jesus from the dead is living in you, he who raised Christ from the dead will also give life to your mortal bodies through his Spirit, who lives in you.

¹²Therefore, brothers, we have an obligation—but it is not to the sinful nature, to live according to it. ¹³For if you live according to the sinful nature, you will die; but if by the Spirit you put to death the misdeeds of the body, you will live, ¹⁴because those who are led by the Spirit of God are sons of God. ¹⁵For you did not receive a spirit that makes you a slave again to fear, but you received the Spirit of sonship. And by him we cry, "Abba, Father." ¹⁶The Spirit himself testifies with our spirit that we are God's children. ¹⁷Now if we are children, then we are heirs—heirs of God and co-heirs with Christ, if indeed we share in his sufferings in order that we may also share in his glory.

To remain in the spiritual haven where condemnation no longer rules, we must have ample help from above, which Paul says is the Holy Spirit. It is very important that disciples have an understanding of the Spirit's work in our behalf. Because this is so important, I want to include a broader NT view of the Holy Spirit's work in our lives.

When we are baptized into a saved relationship with Christ, the Spirit comes to indwell us (Acts 2:38, 5:32). According to Galatians 4:6, he is sent into our hearts by God because we became children of God, thus signifying this new relationship (tie this in with Galatians 3:26-27). Back in John 7:37-39, Jesus had promised this indwelling. Several blessings are connected with it. First, the Spirit is our seal (2 Corinthians 1:21-22, Ephesians 1:13). A seal was an official sign of ownership. When we become Christians, God stamps us as his property! The world may not be able to tell who is a child of God simply by looking, but the spirit world now can.

Second, the Spirit is the deposit of our inheritance (2 Corinthians 5:5, Ephesians 1:14). The deposit here carries the idea of earnest money put down for a purchase, as in a pledge that the full amount will be paid at the proper time. Therefore, the Spirit is God's deposit in us, guaranteeing our future blessings with him (Philippians 3:20-21).

Third, he strengthens us (Ephesians 3:14-21), which is more than being strengthened by the Word (which definitely strengthens us). He also helps us to follow through with our convictions. Of course, he will not force us to do right against our will to do otherwise, but he will strengthen us to do what we really want to do for God. Once I was jogging a much longer distance than I ever had before, and near the end of the run, I came to a formidable hill. When I was tempted to give up, a friend ran behind me with his hand in the middle of my back pushing me. Two things were true: (1) Without his help, I would not have finished. (2) Had I quit running, he could not have helped me, but because I was trying, he could assist me in completing the run. Similarly, the Spirit assists us to complete what we could not complete without his helpful and vital "push."

Fourth, he aids us in godly living. Just knowing that he dwells in me keeps me from wanting to sin (1 Corinthians 6:19-20), for where I go, he goes! Galatians 5 tells us that we "live" by the Spirit in a number of ways: by refusing to gratify the desires of the sinful nature (vv16-17); by being freed from a legalistic, works orientation (v18); by avoiding a life directed by the sinful nature (vv19-21); by developing the fruit of the Spirit (vv22-23); by crucifying the sinful nature (v24); by keeping in step with the Spirit (v25); and by maintaining loving relationships with our brothers (v26).

Romans 8 also promises that, as we set our minds on spiritual living, the Spirit helps us control our minds and lives for God. We have life and peace (v6); our Spirit is alive (v10); life is given to our mortal bodies (v11); we put to death the misdeeds of the body (v13); we are led by the Spirit (v14); we have a Spirit of sonship, not fear (v15); we have the assurance of salvation (vv16-17); and he intercedes for us (vv26-27). The Holy Spirit is vitally concerned about every aspect of our lives. He loves us. He cares how we feel. He intercedes because he is an Encourager (Acts 9:31) and a Counselor to us (John 14:16-18). In that latter role, he joins Jesus in speaking on our behalf (1 John 2:1).

Fifth, the Spirit acts providentially for us, often leading in ways that are very delightful to us, as we are led directly into the blessings of God. However, he also leads us into the desert of trials! (Matthew 4:1). In this gospel context, Jesus was thus led right after a time of great commitment to God's will. Do not be surprised when spiritual mountaintops seem to be followed by some rather intense valleys. Passages like Lamentations 3:38 inform us that everything that happens to us is either directly *caused* by God or at the least *allowed* by him.[1] Rest assured that all the pain that he allows into our lives is designed to strengthen and help us, never to harm us. The key is to trust God no matter what occurs (Romans 8:31-39) and to decide to be thankful *in* (not necessarily *for*) all circumstances (1 Thessalonians 5:16-18).

According to verse 15, by the Spirit our fears give way to the security produced by having God as our adopted Father—Abba, Father. "Abba" is an Aramaic term of endearment, not unlike our English "Daddy." In thinking about this relationship, the words of Psalm 131:2 come to mind: "But I have stilled and quieted my soul; like a weaned child with its mother, like a weaned child is my soul within me." God is to us the perfect Parent, embodying the love of father and mother, with perfect love driving out fear (1 John 4:18). Surely this is such a key idea in the crescendo of Romans 8. We who were enemies of God (chapter 5) are now God's children and able to cry "Abba." Amazing!

The Hope of Resurrection (Romans 8:18-25)

> [18]I consider that our present sufferings are not worth comparing with the glory that will be revealed in us. [19]The creation waits in eager expectation for the sons of God to be revealed. [20]For the creation was subjected to frustration, not by its own choice, but by the will of the one who subjected it, in hope [21]that the creation itself will be liberated from its bondage to decay and brought into the glorious freedom of the children of God.
>
> [22]We know that the whole creation has been groaning as in the pains of childbirth right up to the present time. [23]Not only so, but we ourselves, who have the firstfruits of the Spirit, groan inwardly as we wait eagerly for our adoption as sons, the redemption of our bodies. [24]For in this hope we were saved. But hope that is seen is no hope at all. Who hopes for what he already has? [25]But if we hope for what we do not yet have, we wait for it patiently.

Next, in showing our freedom from condemnation, Paul describes the hope of resurrection that we enjoy (vv18-25). This hope changes our view of suffering. "The creation" here has been viewed by different Biblical students in different ways: some take it to mean mankind generally, but the non-Christian world would hardly be waiting eagerly for the sons of God to be revealed (v19). Some take it to mean the new creation, the church, but then what would be the difference between the creation and the "sons of God" (v19) or "we ourselves"? (vv22-23). Some take it to refer to the physical creation, which would mean that personal attributes would be applied to the creation much the same way as in OT picturesque language (see Psalm 96:11-13, 98:7-9 for examples). All things considered, this view has the most to commend it, for even the physical creation was designed by God to serve in training and preparing humanity spiritually for eternity with God.

Regardless of our interpretation of "the creation" here, the practical message is that hope causes us to persevere through our sufferings with patience. However, this hope causes inward dissatisfaction with this present world (v23). The level of dissatisfaction is indicated by the phrase "groan inwardly." Although we should be upbeat and rejoicing Christians, we are still merely sojourners passing through this world en route to the real world of eternity. To expect that this life be completely fulfilling is to expect the impossible and the un-Biblical. On the other hand, our discontentment must be based on our desire to be with God rather than on the frustrations produced by a materialistic, worldly focus!

The Perfect Providence of God (Romans 8:26-30)

> ²⁶*In the same way, the Spirit helps us in our weakness. We do not know what we ought to pray for, but the Spirit himself intercedes for us with groans that words cannot express.* ²⁷*And he who searches our hearts knows the mind of the Spirit, because the Spirit intercedes for the saints in accordance with God's will.*
>
> ²⁸*And we know that in all things God works for the good of those who love him, who have been called according to his purpose.* ²⁹*For those God foreknew he also predestined to be conformed to the likeness of his Son, that he might be the firstborn among many brothers.* ³⁰*And those he predestined, he also called; those he called, he also justified; those he justified, he also glorified.*

According to verses 26-30, we have the perfect providence of God to guide our future paths. The Holy Spirit intercedes for us (vv26-27) *especially* when we are spiritually weak (far different from what most people think). And then God works for our good in all things (vv28-30). Of course, all things are not good, but still God uses them for our good if we respond with faith to the challenges. The goal of all that God does in our lives is not to make us happy at the moment, but to make us like his Son! This is the good for which he works. We have been predestined, called, justified and glorified. Predestination means that God laid out a plan to offer up Christ and then bless all who would respond to this plan with faith. It means that God determined the plan but not the man—as an individual. In other words, God did not arbitrarily choose certain individuals to be saved and others to be lost. He loves every person profoundly, deeply desiring their repentance (2 Peter 3:9) and their salvation (1 Timothy 2:4).

The Biblical teaching of predestination is far different from the Calvinistic teaching of the same.[2] An illustration from everyday life should help. A schoolteacher prepares a syllabus, or plan, which predetermines that some students will make As, others will make Bs, and so forth, even before he meets his students. Depending on how these students *respond* to these plans, they are in that sense predestined to make specific grades. God himself knows how a given person will respond in advance, but the person still has the freedom to make his choice, because God treats everyone impartially. As difficult as it may be for humans to grasp how the foreknowledge of God and the free will of man interrelate, the Bible places the two principles side by side. (See Acts 2:23 for a classic example.) For example, a person on top of a building may see two cars traveling at a high rate of speed toward each other at the same corner and *know* that their speed and direction is going to ensure that they crash—but his knowledge from "on high" in no way would *cause* the wreck.

Note the following Biblical passages that help explain how predestination practically works in our lives. God calls us by the gospel (2 Thessalonians 2:13-14) to which we just respond in order to be chosen (Matthew 22:1-14). The background of the parable in Matthew 22 is that all invited guests were given a garment to wear when they arrived at the wedding feast. Therefore, the person without the garment had no one to blame but himself for not accepting it. Similarly, God offers us the *opportunity* to be clothed with Christ (Galatians 3:27, Romans 13:14), and if we do not accept his provisions, we have no one to blame but ourselves! God votes for us, Satan votes against us, but we have the deciding vote—the *choice* to be *chosen* is ours! He justifies those who do accept his offer of salvation in Christ with a *just-as-if-I'd*-never-sinned blessing. He also glorifies us—in the *present*, not simply in heaven (Ephesians 2:6-7).

The Absolute Assurance of God's Love (Romans 8:31-39)

> [31] *What, then, shall we say in response to this? If God is for us, who can be against us?* [32] *He who did not spare his own Son, but gave him up for us all—how will he not also, along with him, graciously give us all things?* [33] *Who*

will bring any charge against those whom God has chosen?
It is God who justifies. [34]*Who is he that condemns? Christ*
Jesus, who died—more than that, who was raised to life—
is at the right hand of God and is also interceding for us.
[35]*Who shall separate us from the love of Christ? Shall*
trouble or hardship or persecution or famine or nakedness
or danger or sword? [36]*As it is written:*

> *"For your sake we face death all day long;*
>   *we are considered as sheep to be slaughtered."*

[37]*No, in all these things we are more than conquerors*
through him who loved us. [38]*For I am convinced that*
neither death nor life, neither angels nor demons, neither
the present nor the future, nor any powers, [39]*neither*
height nor depth, nor anything else in all creation, will be
able to separate us from the love of God that is in Christ
Jesus our Lord.

Finally in Romans 8, we are given the absolute assurance of
God's love, from which nothing can separate us (vv31-39). With
God on our side, nothing else really matters (vv31-34). Satan will
accuse us and is certainly against us, but the idea is that we
cannot be *successfully* opposed. If God gave Jesus for us, surely he
will not hold back on any other blessing that we need. Jesus, as
our high priest, joins the Holy Spirit in interceding for us (Hebrews
2:14-18, 4:14-16, 7:23-25). To the disciple who holds on to God,
nothing in this life, no matter how bad, will ever separate him
from the love of Christ (vv35-39). Years ago, I heard the following
story that should help us see the power in all this.

A Parable: The Advocate

When I was a little boy two years of age, my mother
died. When I was four, my father died. I had to live one
place and then another, and I was a sinner. I was going
to turn fourteen years old the tenth of next March. But
now it was Christmastime, and I was caught in sin, put
under arrest and dragged to court.
    I did not cry this time. I had already cried all the
tears out of my head. I tried to look at the judge. I felt so

guilty. I didn't have any friends, and I was miserable. The courtroom was packed with people. They looked at me, and then at the judge. Their faces seemed to say, "Judge, give him the full penalty of the law and save us the trouble later on." I felt as though the whole world was down on me.

In a short while, a court clerk stood up and said, "This court is open."

The judge said to a lawyer, "I appoint you to take this boy's case." He walked through the crowd, pushed the policeman aside, and took me into a room. I sank into a corner. I thought he was going to drag me to execution, and then I saw tears under his eyelashes. He sat down and slipped his arm around me. It was the most tender touch I ever felt and it drew me to him.

"My little friend, are you guilty?" he asked. I could not have lied to him to save the world. He gave me a little squeeze.

I said, "Yes, sir, I am guilty of this and a whole lot more that they don't know about." I was in for a clean breast of it. When I looked at him I could not lie. I had found a friend. I feel his hand yet. Oh, it was a wonderful touch to an orphan boy.

He said, "Do you think you had better confess 'guilty' and throw yourself on the mercy of the court?" I didn't know what that meant, but I thought if he would throw me it would be alright.

I said, "Please, sir, throw me on the mercy of the court." He put his hand on my head, and I put out my dirty fingers and grabbed his coat. The feeling came to me that if I could hang onto his coat, he would pull me through.

He came to the judge and said, "If it please, your honor, it has been my privilege to practice before this bar for many years. I have noticed that when the ends of justice can be secured and society protected, it has been your honor's custom to show mercy. I stand here with this trembling orphan child, without father or mother, home or friend, to beg your honor's mercy. His heart is broken. He readily confesses his sin. He pleads for forgiveness."

I grabbed some more coat. I thought that was a great speech, but it was just the introduction. He spoke until silence filled every mouth. He spoke until the most beautiful language filled every corner of the court. He spoke until old men wept. He spoke until my policeman was brushing tears from his cheeks. He said, "If you will show compassion on this orphan child, I pledge, your honor, to look after his education and his upbringing, and give society a useful and productive citizen. I want to adopt him for my very own." He spoke until my heart nearly burst within me for love and admiration for my friend. If I could just put my ragged sleeves around his neck and kiss him just one time, they could have taken me out and hanged me, and I would have died happy.

Then the greatest shock of all came. He spoke again to the judge and said, "Father." (That shot through me like a bolt from the blue. The judge had appointed his own son to plead for me; surely he would have mercy on me.) "Father," he continued, "the intensity of my love for my little client comes from the fact that he is my brother." (I wasn't much for mathematics, but I could see at once that if the judge on the bench was the father of my attorney and the attorney was my brother, then the judge was my father too. I gave a shout...I made a leap.) Then the judge stood up and said, "Rejoice, for the lost is found, and the dead is alive!"

✠

Though we have sinned and fallen short of God's glory, there is no condemnation for us who are in Christ Jesus. The Spirit of God dwells in us. We are being transformed into the likeness of the Son. God is our Abba and nothing can separate us from his love. The prodigals have come home, and the Father has thrown a banquet for us and will never let us go. Believe it? Yes. Totally grasp it? Impossible! But try we will, as Paul prayed that we might in Ephesians 3:16-19:

> *I pray that out of his glorious riches he may strengthen you with power through his Spirit in your inner being, so that*

*Christ may dwell in your hearts through faith. And I pray
that you, being rooted and established in love, may have
power, together with all the saints, to grasp how wide and
long and high and deep is the love of Christ, and to know
this love that surpasses knowledge—that you may be filled
to the measure of all the fullness of God.*

Notes

1. This material on the Holy Spirit was first published in my book
Revolution! The World-Changing Church in the Book of Acts (Billerica, Mass.:
Discipleship Publications International, 1998) chapter 2, 40-41.

2. For more detail on the tenets of Calvinism, see my book *Prepared to
Answer* (Billerica, Mass.: Discipleship Publications International, 1995, 1998),
chapter 7.

III

Righteousness and the Exclusion of Israel

9

God's Right to Make His Choices

Romans 9

After carefully developing the doctrine of justification by grace through faith in chapters 1-8, Paul, in what might be considered a long parenthesis that continues from chapter 9 through chapter 11, now addresses the issue of physical Israel. Apparently he knew that some would be troubled and would ask: If the Jews were used by God as a nation in bringing salvation to the world (by producing the Messiah), why were the large majority of them not in his kingdom?

Paul explains that the problem is not God's love, nor even his love as a fellow Israelite—the problem was the Jews' reaction to a crucified Messiah. As always in God's dealings with man, it boils down to the issue of *choice*.

God created us as humans, which means that we have the ability and the freedom to choose. That freedom would not be freedom unless we could choose either the good or the bad. When we exercise this freedom in the wrong way, God does everything possible to persuade us otherwise, but he will never remove our freedom in the process. Sadly, most Jews chose to reject the Messiah who did not fit their mold of what they thought a Messiah should be. Of course, Jesus fulfilled OT prophecy perfectly, but Jewish expectations were more based on traditions than Scripture. However, neither God nor Paul had given up trying to reach them. With the skilled pen of a rabbi, Paul masterfully used Jewish history to reach out with the heart of God to hearts that were hardened to the gospel. Maybe there was yet hope! With that thought burning inside, Paul begins.

Paul's Love for His Jewish Brothers (Romans 9:1-3)

> $^{9:1}$I speak the truth in Christ—I am not lying, my con-
> science confirms it in the Holy Spirit—^{2}I have great sorrow
> and unceasing anguish in my heart. ^{3}For I could wish that
> I myself were cursed and cut off from Christ for the sake of
> my brothers, those of my own race....

Paul begins by expressing his own intense love for his coun-
trymen. He assures the readers that he is being truthful about this,
for no one was more hard-line in his preaching to Jewish audi-
ences than was Paul. Read Acts 28:23-28 to get a feel for the
power of his convictions and the directness with which he spoke.
He was a great imitator of Jesus, who said: "Those whom I love I
rebuke and discipline. So be earnest, and repent" (Revelation
3:19). Those with soft hearts respond to strong preaching in one
way and those with hard hearts in another. Hence Paul's assurance that even when he spoke the truth strongly, it was out of
deep love (Ephesians 4:15).

Paul asserts that he lived with the burden of their spiritual
rejection and in fact would be willing to be lost if that would save
them. I can only wish that my love for the lost equaled that of
Paul. Allow yourself to sit quietly and contemplate that possibility
in your own life—think about being lost for eternity, and think
about who you love enough to go to hell for! Paul's statement
about having constant sorrow and anguish does catch us off
guard, because we think of him as being such a positive, upbeat
thinker. After all, he is the one who said to rejoice always
(Philippians 4:4; 1 Thessalonians 5:16). Even though he said that
and did that, he still had "unceasing anguish" in his heart over his
lost brothers. This passage shows us some of what "groaning"
meant in Romans 8:22.

Obviously, the anguish and the rejoicing exist together. Our
pain is produced by others' lack of relationship with God, and our
joy is produced by the relationship all who are in Christ have with
him. Our sinful tendency is to let things of this world rob us of personal joy and weaken our convictions about the plight of non-
Christians. God help us to repent and become like Paul!

God's Love in Making Choices (Romans 9:4-18)

⁴...the people of Israel. Theirs is the adoption as sons; theirs the divine glory, the covenants, the receiving of the law, the temple worship and the promises. ⁵Theirs are the patriarchs, and from them is traced the human ancestry of Christ, who is God over all, forever praised! Amen.

⁶It is not as though God's word had failed. For not all who are descended from Israel are Israel. ⁷Nor because they are his descendants are they all Abraham's children. On the contrary, "It is through Isaac that your offspring will be reckoned." ⁸In other words, it is not the natural children who are God's children, but it is the children of the promise who are regarded as Abraham's offspring. ⁹For this was how the promise was stated: "At the appointed time I will return, and Sarah will have a son."

¹⁰Not only that, but Rebekah's children had one and the same father, our father Isaac. ¹¹Yet, before the twins were born or had done anything good or bad—in order that God's purpose in election might stand: ¹²not by works but by him who calls—she was told, "The older will serve the younger." ¹³Just as it is written: "Jacob I loved, but Esau I hated."

¹⁴What then shall we say? Is God unjust? Not at all! ¹⁵For he says to Moses,

> *"I will have mercy on whom I have mercy,*
>   *and I will have compassion on whom I have*
>   *compassion."*

¹⁶It does not, therefore, depend on man's desire or effort, but on God's mercy. ¹⁷For the Scripture says to Pharaoh: "I raised you up for this very purpose, that I might display my power in you and that my name might be proclaimed in all the earth." ¹⁸Therefore God has mercy on whom he wants to have mercy, and he hardens whom he wants to harden.

God had clearly loved and blessed the Jewish nation throughout their history (vv4-5). Of all the people on the face of the earth, they had been most blessed. Here Paul lists seven things that were unique to their nation. In light of this, how could they question God's love? What else could he have done to win their hearts and move them to repentance by his kindness? (Romans 2:4).

However, he had always made choices in his dealings with Israel, most of which the Jews accepted (vv6-13). In fact, they gloried in them as they recounted them with great pleasure and approval. Their very lineage showed God's choices, and none of them would have argued that the choices were poor ones. But their sacred history demonstrated clearly that it had never been simply an issue of physical descent. Abraham had two sons, but only one was chosen. Isaac also had two sons, and only one of them was chosen.

The allegation that God loved Jacob and hated Esau is somewhat shocking at first glance. But this is a quote from Malachi 1:2-3, referring to the nations of Israel and Edom respectively, and thus the term "hate" applies primarily to a nation. God chose Jacob, who had character flaws of his own, but who became a man of faith after he responded to the Lord's discipline. Sometimes Biblical writers describe Jacob as negatively as his brother Esau, which suggests that God's choice had no moral basis. But the passage of time showed that Jacob had the more righteous heart. However, the point of Paul's argument is that God had the *right* to make these choices.

God's deliverance of his people from Egypt showed other choices—ones that the people had always readily accepted. Moses was especially blessed to catch a glimpse of God that no one else was privileged to see (Exodus 33:18-23). Pharaoh, on the other hand, was hardened by God. What does that mean? Simply this: God "hardened" Pharaoh through his commands and Pharaoh's free will to choose. Back in Exodus, the text says a number of times that God hardened Pharaoh's heart and a number of times that Pharaoh hardened his own heart. God's word hardens some hearts and softens others, depending on the type of heart that is responding to his word. For example the same sun hardens clay and melts butter. But again, the thrust of this passage in Romans is that God has the right to do what he pleases. Thankfully, he pleases to always do what is righteous—that which allows men to make their own moral choices.

God's Choices Were Always Right (Romans 9:19-33)

[19]*One of you will say to me: "Then why does God still blame us? For who resists his will?"* [20]*But who are you, O man, to talk back to God? "Shall what is formed say to him who formed it, 'Why did you make me like this?'"* [21]*Does not the potter have the right to make out of the same lump of clay some pottery for noble purposes and some for common use?*

[22]*What if God, choosing to show his wrath and make his power known, bore with great patience the objects of his wrath—prepared for destruction?* [23]*What if he did this to make the riches of his glory known to the objects of his mercy, whom he prepared in advance for glory—* [24]*even us, whom he also called, not only from the Jews but also from the Gentiles?* [25]*As he says in Hosea:*

> *"I will call them 'my people' who are not my*
> > *people;*
> > *and I will call her 'my loved one' who is not my*
> > *loved one,"* [26]*and,*

> *"It will happen that in the very place where it was*
> > *said to them,*
> *'You are not my people,'*
> *they will be called 'sons of the living God.'"*

[27]*Isaiah cries out concerning Israel:*

> *"Though the number of the Israelites be like the sand*
> > *by the sea,*
> > *only the remnant will be saved.*
> [28]*For the Lord will carry out*
> > *his sentence on earth with speed and finality."*

[29]*It is just as Isaiah said previously:*

> *"Unless the Lord Almighty*
> > *had left us descendants,*
> *we would have become like Sodom,*
> > *we would have been like Gomorrah."*

30What then shall we say? That the Gentiles, who did not pursue righteousness, have obtained it, a righteousness that is by faith; 31but Israel, who pursued a law of righteousness, has not attained it. 32Why not? Because they pursued it not by faith but as if it were by works. They stumbled over the "stumbling stone." 33As it is written:

*"See, I lay in Zion a stone that causes men to
    stumble
and a rock that makes them fall,
and the one who trusts in him will never be put to
    shame."*

God is always God, and he is always right. He is the potter, and man is only clay. Obviously, the potter can do what he wants with his own clay! Romans 9 is a much-used chapter by advocates of Calvinist theology in their attempt to show unconditional election and predestination, and the potter and clay illustration is a favorite as they try to bolster such a belief. The clay has nothing to do with how the potter chooses to shape it, we are told by them. However, similar potter and clay passages show that while God has the right to do what he wants, the clay has *a choice* in the outcome of the shaping (see especially Jeremiah 18:1-10). An important NT passage that uses the potter and the clay analogy and emphasizes the free will of man is 2 Timothy 2:20-21:

In a large house there are articles not only of gold and silver, but also of wood and clay; some are for noble purposes and some for ignoble. If a man cleanses himself from the latter, he will be an instrument for noble purposes, made holy, useful to the Master and prepared to do any good work.

The sovereignty of God and the free choice of man run concurrently all through the Scriptures (again, see Acts 2:23 for a classic text). As difficult as it may be for our minds to harmonize the two, we cannot throw out either part of the equation. God's foreknowledge and man's choices, complete with man's total responsibility, are not mutually exclusive. And that God knows in advance what someone is going to do in no way rules out free moral agency nor forces him to do it. Just because two things seem contradictory from our limited perspective does not mean that they are. My friend Douglas Jacoby tells me that there was a time when scientists thought light consisted of particles. Later its wave nature was discovered. It seemed counter-intuitive to think that it could be both, but now we refer to light as a particle-wave. So it is with the sovereignty of God and the free will of man. Both are true.

In Romans 9:20-21, we see that getting angry and blaming God is totally out of place. It is true that the psalmists often questioned God as an emotional reaction to pain, but they did so as a part of the process of surrendering to God. A given psalm may begin with such questioning, but in all but one case (Psalm 88), the writer had worked through it and settled out in faith by the end of the psalm. That sort of questioning is acceptable to God, because as a good Father, he wants his children to honestly deal with their emotions. On the other hand, Job went much beyond an initial emotional reaction. He intellectually built a case against God over a sustained period of time, and he had to learn the lesson mentioned here in Romans 9 the hard way. Therefore, let us work through our pain and then trust and surrender to the God who knows all things and loves us unconditionally.

In verses 22-29, Paul makes a point from the Old Testament that only a remnant in the Jewish nation had ever really followed God heart and soul. How could they argue with their own history? As mentioned previously, there were really two OT election processes working at the same time, the physical and the spiritual, but the Jews mistakenly assumed that the former guaranteed the latter. They could not have been more wrong, and their own prophets had clearly made that point, if the Jews had but listened.

✛

The fact that becomes more obvious in Paul's line of reasoning is that Israel simply made the wrong choice. Israel's response to Christ and to the cross revealed the nature of their hearts (vv30-33). They pursued the law that was designed to lead them to righteousness in Christ, but they sought it by performance, not by faith. Hence, they stumbled at the idea that they were so sinful that God had to become a man and die for them. The cross was pure foolishness to them (1 Corinthians 1:18-25). They did not understand God's way of making men right with himself—grace through faith—and sought to establish their own path to being right with God—legalism. Their rejection of Jesus as the Messiah showed how entrenched legalism was in their hearts. The true Jews, like the three thousand who were baptized on the day of Pentecost (Acts 2:41), obviously had very different hearts, the kind we must also have.

10

Israel's Lack of True Faith
Romans 10

Romans 9 made the point that God had the right to make the choices that he did, including the choice not to bend his rules for the physical Israelites. Romans 10 argues that the real problem is Israel, for most Israelites had simply made the wrong choice by deciding to reject Jesus. That rejection was not God's fault, and certainly not his will. It could and should have been different. Romans 11 will go on to show that even though the choice had been wrong up until then, it could in fact be reversed. God's outstretched hand has not been pulled back; he was and is still willing and anxious to accept the Jews, but only if they exercise true faith. Zeal they had, but faith they did not. Hence Paul addresses this issue head-on.

Israel Had a Zeal for God (Romans 10:1-4)

> ^{10:1}*Brothers, my heart's desire and prayer to God for the Israelites is that they may be saved.* ²*For I can testify about them that they are zealous for God, but their zeal is not based on knowledge.* ³*Since they did not know the righteousness that comes from God and sought to establish their own, they did not submit to God's righteousness.* ⁴*Christ is the end of the law so that there may be righteousness for everyone who believes.*

The Israelites were filled with zeal for God, but it was misdirected zeal. Christ was the *end*, the aim, the fulfillment, of the Law of Moses—it all pointed to salvation in him. From this passage, it is obvious that we cannot be saved outside of a true relationship with God through Jesus Christ. Belief in Jehovah did not save those who did not accept Christ. Spiritual zeal did not save them either. The Bible is clear about this matter of salvation: No one can come to the Father except through Jesus (John 14:6), and no salvation can be found in anyone else (Acts 4:12). If these statements are viewed as narrow-minded, so be it, for Jesus himself said that the way of salvation was narrow! (Matthew 7:13-14, 21).

Many people reason that one religion is as good as any other, under the premise that the goal of all of them is to persuade people to be good. Certainly, God does want us to be good and to do good. However, the key difference in Christianity and other religions is that Jesus says that we are not good and cannot consistently do good in and of ourselves. In our flesh lives no good thing (Romans 7:18). Apart from Christ, we can do nothing (John 15:5). "There is no one who does good, not even one" (Romans 3:12). Sure, even unbelievers are capable of acts of kindness and compassion; but God's standard of "good" is himself, and our hearts are far from being like his. God's approach is to show us our sinful nature and to convict us of our sin. Once we see that we are not good in ourselves, we can repent, trust in the righteousness of Christ and become Christians. Then, we receive the Holy Spirit, who enables us to be good and to do good. As Romans 8:4 says, "The righteous requirements of the law might be fully met in us, who do not live according to the sinful nature but according to the Spirit."

Humanism, by this or whatever other names it is known, has failed for centuries and is failing in our day. The way of man is simply not in himself (Jeremiah 10:23). But no religion outside what is described in the Bible approaches it in the way that God does. Therefore, no other religion addresses the hearts of men and changes the hearts of men the way that God does via his word. Christianity is decidedly not just another religion!

Righteousness Was Readily Available (Romans 10:5-15)

> [5]Moses describes in this way the righteousness that is by the law: "The man who does these things will live by them." [6]But the righteousness that is by faith says: "Do not say in your heart, 'Who will ascend into heaven?'" (that is, to bring Christ down) [7]"or 'Who will descend into the deep?'" (that is, to bring Christ up from the dead). [8]But

*what does it say? "The word is near you; it is in your
mouth and in your heart," that is, the word of faith we are
proclaiming: *[9]*That if you confess with your mouth, "Jesus
is Lord," and believe in your heart that God raised him
from the dead, you will be saved. *[10]*For it is with your heart
that you believe and are justified, and it is with your mouth
that you confess and are saved. *[11]*As the Scripture says,
"Anyone who trusts in him will never be put to shame."
*[12]*For there is no difference between Jew and Gentile—the
same Lord is Lord of all and richly blesses all who call on
him, *[13]*for, "Everyone who calls on the name of the Lord
will be saved."*

*[14]How, then, can they call on the one they have not
believed in? And how can they believe in the one of whom
they have not heard? And how can they hear without
someone preaching to them? *[15]*And how can they preach
unless they are sent? As it is written, "How beautiful are the
feet of those who bring good news!"*

In Romans 10:5-15, Paul proceeds to demonstrate that the
spiritual needs of the Jews could have been met, for righteousness
was readily available. The hard part had already been done—
Christ died and was resurrected. The word of faith is simple to
obey: Simply believe, confess and call on him.

Sadly, Romans 10:9-10 is often quoted as proof that baptism
is not part of the salvation process. However, a proof-text out of
context is a *pretext!* These verses cannot be used to exclude
baptism from God's plan to save us, for several reasons. First,
chapter 10 follows chapter 6, and in that chapter, baptism is
clearly taught as part of dying to sin and being raised to begin a
new life. That is clearly a salvation text and surely Paul had not
forgotten what he had just written there! Second, "trusts" in verse
11 and "call on him" in verse 12 go further than simply believing
and confessing. The progression in verses 14-15 is preaching,
hearing, believing and calling. Calling on the name of the Lord
includes baptism, as may be readily seen in Acts 2:21 and 38,
and also in Acts 22:16. In Acts 2:21, Peter quotes from Joel 2:32,
which reads: "And everyone who calls on the name of the Lord
will be saved." When the people asked, in essence, just how to
do that, Peter told them to repent and be baptized (Acts 2:37-38).

Acts 22:16 is even clearer, as Paul was told to "get up, be baptized and wash your sins away, calling on his name."

In Romans 10:9-10 Paul talks about the Jews who failed to accept Christ and addresses the reasons for that rejection. He makes the point, beginning in verse 5, that the righteousness which comes by faith is neither a complex issue nor an unreachable goal. God has already done the difficult work by sending his Son to the cross. In response to what he did, we need to accept him as Lord and Messiah. This was the challenge to the Jews. Being baptized was not a hard concept for them. Proselytes to Judaism were customarily baptized as an initiation rite into Judaism. It had been a part of John's ministry, and large numbers of Jews had received it from his hands. Matthew 3:5-6 says,

> *People went out to him from Jerusalem and all Judea and the whole region of the Jordan. Confessing their sins, they were baptized by him in the Jordan River.*

Therefore, Paul had no reason to mention baptism again in this chapter because it was not their stumbling block.

The problem that the Jews did have was to accept Jesus as the Messiah and to then make this crucified Jew from despised Nazareth their Lord and King. Now *that* was a challenge! This background explains why Paul worded the passage as he did.

In a related vein, the problem with Gentile acceptance of the gospel was repentance. Therefore, Luke, a book written by a Gentile for Gentiles, focused on that need all through his Gospel. In fact, his account of the Great Commission only mentions repentance:

> *He told them, "This is what is written: The Christ will suffer and rise from the dead on the third day, and repentance and forgiveness of sins will be preached in his name to all nations, beginning at Jerusalem." (Luke 24:46-47)*

Luke's failure to specifically name faith in this account does not mean that he was excluding it from the conversion process. He was simply focusing on the Gentiles' greatest challenge. And Luke's approach follows exactly the same principle used by Paul in Romans 10: Address the key need of the intended audience.

Many religious people have great difficulty allowing *conditions* to accompany the grace God offers to man. But conditions do not violate grace unless we begin to trust the conditions rather than the grace itself. For example, in Joshua 1:2, God *gave* the city of Jericho to the Israelites (clearly a gift of grace!). Then in the following verses, God attached some very specific conditions of obedience to his promise of grace. After the people had complied with the conditions, they received the promised city. Yet, the victory was clearly one of faith and not of works, for Hebrews 11:30 states, "By faith the walls of Jericho fell, after the people had marched around them for seven days." It is never a question of *what* saves us—it is faith; but it is a question of *when* faith saves. It saves us when we have responded with trusting attitudes to the conditions that God has placed on his graceful offers. Clearly this is the case with baptism!

Israel's Rejection and Gentiles' Acceptance Was Foretold (Romans 10:16-21)

> [16]But not all the Israelites accepted the good news. For Isaiah says, "Lord, who has believed our message?" [17]Consequently, faith comes from hearing the message, and the message is heard through the word of Christ. [18]But I ask: Did they not hear? Of course they did:
>
> > "Their voice has gone out into all the earth,
> > their words to the ends of the world."
>
> [19]Again I ask: Did Israel not understand? First, Moses says,
>
> > "I will make you envious by those who are not a
> > nation;
> > I will make you angry by a nation that has no
> > understanding."
>
> [20]And Isaiah boldly says,
>
> > "I was found by those who did not seek me;
> > I revealed myself to those who did not ask for me."
>
> [21]But concerning Israel he says,

Gentiles are undeserving, and oblivious! Tripped over a gold mine!

Israel's underway, yet knowing

> "All day long I have held out my hands
> to a disobedient and obstinate people."

As in the ending of Romans 9, Paul makes two basic points: only a remnant of Israel had ever responded in faith to God; and the inclusion of the Gentiles was foretold by Israel's own prophets. The bulk of the Jews rejected Christ because they did not accept the words of Scripture that they supposedly cherished like no other. They had possessed the message for centuries, but they had misinterpreted it by reading into it what they wanted to see. If we come to the Bible to prove a point that we already have decided upon, we are wasting time opening it up. We will see only what our hearts are prepared to see. Some people can hear a sermon and only cling to the one or two things that they agree with, while the other things go right through both ears without penetrating either the mind or the heart.

✠

The message, says Paul, comes through hearing the word of Christ. Certainly the Old Testament was all about Christ, for he himself said to the Jews:

> You diligently study the Scriptures because you think that
> by them you possess eternal life. These are the Scriptures
> that testify about me. (John 5:39)

As far back as Moses, their rejection was cause for God to announce that he would use another nation to provoke them to envy (Deuteronomy 32:21). (Paul will make much use in Romans 11 of this envy-provoking idea.) Then other prophets, such as Isaiah, added their voice to the same message. Israel could not claim that Paul's argument was a new revelation to them; they had only to read their own prophets. The fact of the matter was what Paul concluded the chapter with: "All day long I have held out my hands to an obstinate people" (Isaiah 65:2). How sad! But for God's apostle, hope springs eternal, and in Romans 11, he continues to try to move the Jews toward faith in Jesus.

11

Israel's Choice Is Not Irreversible
Romans 11

As Paul brings his line of reasoning about the Jews and the new covenant to a conclusion, he corrects attitudes of both those with Jewish and Gentile backgrounds. The Jews thought that God had excluded them with some ulterior, negative motive, which was certainly not true. His invitation is always open to anyone who will hear. The NT message closes out with such an invitation:

> The Spirit and the bride say, "Come!" And let him who hears say, "Come!" Whoever is thirsty, let him come; and whoever wishes, let him take the free gift of the water of life. (Revelation 22:17)

This is forevermore the heart of God for everyone, and certainly for the Jews, with whom he shared so much history and so many memories.

By this point in Paul's arguments, the Gentiles were running the risk of becoming self-righteous and puffed up about their inclusion in God's kingdom. Thus, they had to be warned. Pride is and always has been looking for ways to get into the nooks and crannies of our hearts. We are all too tempted to think more highly of ourselves than we ought to think (Romans 12:3), for many reasons. We can be prideful about our salvation, the fact that we chose Jesus when most do not. But why did we choose him? Surely not because we are good, for no one is good. Everything about our salvation is a matter of grace. Acts 11:18 informs us that even our repentance is by God's grace. Why was I open to the gospel? I have wondered this so many times, but the answer has to simply be God's inscrutable grace. Paul, the apostle of grace, makes sure that those on both sides of the issues get what they need in Romans 11, whether encouragement or correction.

Only a Remnant (Romans 11:1-10)

> [11:1]I ask then: Did God reject his people? By no means! I am an Israelite myself, a descendant of Abraham, from the tribe of Benjamin. [2]God did not reject his people, whom he foreknew. Don't you know what the Scripture says in the passage about Elijah—how he appealed to God against Israel: [3]"Lord, they have killed your prophets and torn down your altars; I am the only one left, and they are trying to kill me"? [4]And what was God's answer to him? "I have reserved for myself seven thousand who have not bowed the knee to Baal." [5]So too, at the present time there is a remnant chosen by grace. [6]And if by grace, then it is no longer by works; if it were, grace would no longer be grace.
>
> [7]What then? What Israel sought so earnestly it did not obtain, but the elect did. The others were hardened, [8]as it is written:
>
> > "God gave them a spirit of stupor,
> >   eyes so that they could not see
> >   and ears so that they could not hear,
> > to this very day."
>
> [9]And David says:
>
> > "May their table become a snare and a trap,
> >   a stumbling block and a retribution for them.
> > [10]May their eyes be darkened so they cannot see,
> >   and their backs be bent forever."

Actually, only a remnant of Israel had ever made the right choices. Paul was an example of those in the remnant in the first century, as were thousands more. In Acts 21:20, James mentioned that thousands were believers at that time in Jerusalem. In Elijah's day, God said that seven thousand had "not bowed the knee to Baal"—and keep in mind that Elijah was a prophet in the northern kingdom, the most godless part of Israel. The ones who did not respond to grace were hardened by their own rejection. As was the case with the hardening of Pharaoh's heart, verse 8 shows that God gave the people a "spirit of stupor." He did this by giving commands of righteousness and giving them the freedom to make choices in their response to these commands, thus revealing the nature of their own hearts.

The same principle is applied by Jesus in his use of parables (Matthew 13:13-16). The lesson that we must gain from this passage in Romans is a realization and appreciation of how God wrote his message in a manner that reveals hearts. Sometimes it's difficult to accept this on a practical level. For example I remember being frustrated once after a study with a non-Christian. The person had dodged the obvious teaching about baptism in order to hold on to a denominational doctrine of salvation. I thought to myself, "If only God had written it another way...then he couldn't dodge it anymore!" Thankfully, I did not go down that path of thinking for long because I thought about how the Word reveals hearts.

God reveals himself to man in two basic ways: through the creation, as Romans 1:20 says, and through the Word. In both cases, God makes himself known—but he does not force us to see things his way. I look at a newborn baby and exclaim, "Isn't God great?" The atheist looks at the same phenomenon and exclaims, "Isn't evolution grand!" Similarly, a Lydia could hear one message and respond in faith (Acts 16), while the Jews about whom Paul wrote could try to kill him for preaching the very same message. The Word can be understood by a person with a heart of faith, but it can be twisted by a person without a heart of humble faith. The writer of Hebrews tells us, "For the word of God is living and active. Sharper than any double-edged sword, it penetrates even to dividing soul and spirit, joints and marrow; it judges the thoughts and attitudes of the heart" (Hebrews 4:12). We must bear in mind that it is through this word that, "Everything is uncovered and laid bare before the eyes of him to whom we must give account" (Hebrews 4:13).

God's Use of Wrong Choices (Romans 11:11-24)

> [11] *Again I ask: Did they stumble so as to fall beyond recovery? Not at all! Rather, because of their transgression,*

salvation has come to the Gentiles to make Israel envious.
[12]But if their transgression means riches for the world, and their loss means riches for the Gentiles, how much greater riches will their fullness bring!

[13]I am talking to you Gentiles. Inasmuch as I am the apostle to the Gentiles, I make much of my ministry [14]in the hope that I may somehow arouse my own people to envy and save some of them. [15]For if their rejection is the reconciliation of the world, what will their acceptance be but life from the dead? [16]If the part of the dough offered as firstfruits is holy, then the whole batch is holy; if the root is holy, so are the branches.

[17]If some of the branches have been broken off, and you, though a wild olive shoot, have been grafted in among the others and now share in the nourishing sap from the olive root, [18]do not boast over those branches. If you do, consider this: You do not support the root, but the root supports you. [19]You will say then, "Branches were broken off so that I could be grafted in." [20]Granted. But they were broken off because of unbelief, and you stand by faith. Do not be arrogant, but be afraid. [21]For if God did not spare the natural branches, he will not spare you either.

[22]Consider therefore the kindness and sternness of God: sternness to those who fell, but kindness to you, provided that you continue in his kindness. Otherwise, you also will be cut off. [23]And if they do not persist in unbelief, they will be grafted in, for God is able to graft them in again. [24]After all, if you were cut out of an olive tree that is wild by nature, and contrary to nature were grafted into a cultivated olive tree, how much more readily will these, the natural branches, be grafted into their own olive tree!

In spite of God's pain over a majority of Jews rejecting Christ, he still intended to use even their *wrong* choices to accomplish good. (And that is a powerful lesson for believers to remember in any age.) Israel's wrong choices and subsequent rejection has ended up being a blessing to the Gentiles. The Jews had Jesus crucified, making salvation available to Jews and Gentiles alike. The Jews also drove Christians out of Jerusalem, which resulted in the Gentiles being able to hear the gospel sooner. Because of the Jews' rejection of the message in each city to which the early missionaries preached, the missionaries then preached to the Gentiles (Acts 13:46). If the Jews' rejection of the gospel ended up blessing the world, then how much more their acceptance would do! Paul hopes that the Gentile inclusion in God's kingdom will provoke the Jews to envy, causing them to reconsider the message of Christ (vv13-14).

This section of the letter to the Romans concludes with a warning to the Gentiles not to be prideful and self-righteous. They had not been a part of the olive root (Judaism) in the first place—they had been merely grafted in by the grace of God. The Jews were cut off because of their faithless rejection of Christ, but they can be grafted back in again if they turn to Jesus in faith.

I have long thought application could be made from this passage to the movement many of us have been part of for the last twenty or thirty years. The original idea of restoring NT Christianity in modern times did not begin with us, but rather with believers in the early nineteenth century. We have built upon their foundation. Most of what I believe to be true from the Bible, I learned while I was a part of what I call the mainline Church of Christ, a development of that earlier movement. I appreciate that learning and the ones who worked to instill it in me. To be sure, in different wings of that movement, the gospel of grace through faith is all but missing. However, I believe that one of the major reasons I left was the disparity between what was taught and what was done. Obviously, they did not teach everything that we do, but the real problem for me was the lack of commitment, the traditionalism, the deadness. Having said that, I still think self-righteousness toward them is absolutely parallel to that of the Gentiles toward the Jews as Paul describes it in Romans 11.

They Still Had Choices to Make (Romans 11:25-36)

> [25]*I do not want you to be ignorant of this mystery, brothers, so that you may not be conceited: Israel has experienced a hardening in part until the full number of the Gentiles has come in.* [26]*And so all Israel will be saved, as it is written:*
>
> > *"The deliverer will come from Zion;*
> > *he will turn godlessness away from Jacob.*

> ^{27}And this is my covenant with them
>   when I take away their sins."

^{28}As far as the gospel is concerned, they are enemies on your account; but as far as election is concerned, they are loved on account of the patriarchs, ^{29}for God's gifts and his call are irrevocable. ^{30}Just as you who were at one time disobedient to God have now received mercy as a result of their disobedience, ^{31}so they too have now become disobedient in order that they too may now receive mercy as a result of God's mercy to you. ^{32}For God has bound all men over to disobedience so that he may have mercy on them all.

> ^{33}Oh, the depth of the riches of the wisdom and
>   knowledge of God!
> How unsearchable his judgments,
>   and his paths beyond tracing out!
> ^{34}"Who has known the mind of the Lord?
>   Or who has been his counselor?"
> ^{35}"Who has ever given to God,
>   that God should repay him?"
> ^{36}For from him and through him and to him are
>   all things.
> To him be the glory forever! Amen.

The motivation and opportunities for future choices are found in verses 25-36. Israel's hardening is only partial, until the "full number" of Gentiles has come in. If their hardening is partial, then it has the possibility of being reversed. And somehow the key to a reversal is the coming in of the full number of Gentiles. But what does this mean? Paul likely was referring to the completion of his own ministry as the apostle to the Gentiles (Galatians 2:7), resulting in more and more Gentiles in the church all over the world. In Romans 15:24, we learn that his missionary plans were not nearly completed, for he planned to go as far as Spain. Once this larger Gentile inclusion had occurred, all Israel could be saved with the help of the envy-provoking process mentioned back in verses 13-14. The word "so" in verse 26 is from the Greek *houtos*, an adverb of manner, meaning "in this way." (Paul refers to the same idea again in Romans 11:31.) Therefore, when the

Jews saw the growing number of Gentiles in the church and the blessings from God that they were enjoying, those with good hearts would be envious enough to humble themselves and reconsider the gospel message. In this way, they would be saved.

Therefore, the "all Israel" refers to those whose hearts would become humble and reconsider. It could not refer to every last Israelite coming to Christ at some future point, for a number of reasons. For starters, the narrow path will never be chosen by a majority from any nation, race or population group (Matthew 7:13-14). Paul had already in this chapter expressed his hope that "some" (not all) would turn to Christ by being provoked to envy (v14).

Even if some future generation of Jews in the majority were to accept Christ (which I do not believe will happen), what comfort would that be to the scores of generations that had already died lost? The key idea of "all Israel" being saved is that of hopeful potential—much like Jesus expressed in John 12:32, when he said, "I...will draw all men to myself" and said in John 13:35, "By this will all men know that you are my disciples."

I mentioned earlier that I see a parallel between our movement and the mainline church regarding our need to avoid self-righteousness like the plague that it is. Another parallel concerns the envy-producing process that Paul referred to. This was precisely what worked with me. I attended an evangelism seminar in March of 1981 and was absolutely amazed at what I saw. One minister asked everyone in the audience of about two thousand to stand if they had been baptized in the past two years. Two things caught my attention immediately: most of the audience stood, and most of them were young. The churches of which I was a part knew nothing of that kind of rapid growth, and most of the members were not young. I was never the same after that defining moment and ultimately decided to become a part of what I had seen. I was provoked to a godly envy and did something about it, praise Jesus! No doubt Paul saw the same phenomenon in his day, just as he hoped and prayed for when he wrote Romans 11.

Note that the quote in Romans 11:26-27 refers to salvation in Christ which became available at the cross and will continue to be available to anyone who will accept the gospel in faith. The only plan of salvation that God has and will have to the end of time is this plan—which must be accepted individually! God still loves the rejecting Jews and wants to save them, for the promises made to the patriarchs still stand.

✠

The chapter concludes with a beautiful doxology (vv 33-36), showing that God's ways are beyond man's ways. It would seem that Paul's reflection on all this causes him to fall down and worship. Though God moves in ways beyond our comprehension, we do know that even bad things, like Israel's rejection, can be used for good ends, even as Romans 8:28 promises. Praise God that he is in control of the world and not we ourselves. Hope does spring eternal!

IV

Righteousness Results in
Real Relationships

12

Real Relationships
Romans 12

In chapters 1-8, Paul developed in a systematic manner the doctrine of justification by grace through faith. Then in chapters 9-11, he applied that doctrine to the then current situation of Judaism, how God viewed the Jews and how he had used them. In chapters 12-16, Paul applies the doctrine to the everyday lives of the disciples—*how should we then live?*

Granting the careful way that Paul developed the doctrine of how we are to be saved and to live, we would expect that Paul would conclude by elaborating on what Jesus said was the bottom line, the *greatest* commandments—to love God and to love our neighbors as ourselves (Matthew 22:36-40). And this he clearly does! Romans 12 tells us that the essence of the new life in Christ is relationships.

Paul develops this theme very systematically. He describes what it means to love God with all our heart, soul, mind and strength (vv1-2). Next, he describes how to love (view) ourselves (vv 3-8). Only when we view ourselves in the right way are we able to view others in the right way. Paul describes what it means to love our neighbors, in the church and out of the church (vv9-21). Hence, Paul discusses the two greatest commandments, with the proper understanding of "self" sandwiched between the two.

A Life of Worship (Romans 12:1-2)

> ^{12:1}*Therefore, I urge you, brothers, in view of God's mercy, to offer your bodies as living sacrifices, holy and pleasing to God—this is your spiritual act of worship. ²Do not conform any longer to the pattern of this world, but be transformed by the renewing of your mind. Then you will*

> *be able to test and approve what God's will is—his good, pleasing and perfect will.*

Our relationship with God is described in terms of the motivation for developing this relationship: God's mercy. Hopefully after the first eleven chapters of Romans we have quite a "view" of that mercy. Then the worship in this relationship is defined as offering "our bodies as living sacrifices" (v1). As the animal sacrifices had to die, so our old self must be crucified with Christ in order for him to now live through us as living sacrifices (Galatians 2:20; 2 Corinthians 5:15). Worship thus is not compartmentalized—it is a seven-days-per-week, twenty-four-hours-per-day response to the mercy of God. And we must worship with reason, not ritual—"spiritual," from *logikos*, means "belonging to reason." The focus in our relationship with God is described by our being transformed, not conformed. "Transformed," from *metamorphoo*, from which we get the English "metamorphosis," means "to change to another form." (See Matthew 17:2 and 2 Corinthians 3:18 for other uses of the word.) It is further shown by our being able to discern his will for us, which in context most likely means that we can understand our gifts and roles in the body, Paul's next topics.

Who Am I and Why Am I Here? (Romans 12:3-8)

> [3]*For by the grace given me I say to every one of you: Do not think of yourself more highly than you ought, but rather think of yourself with sober judgment, in accordance with the measure of faith God has given you.* [4]*Just as each of us has one body with many members, and these members do not all have the same function,* [5]*so in Christ we who are many form one body, and each member belongs to all the others.* [6]*We have different gifts, according to the grace given us. If a man's gift is prophesying, let him use it in proportion to his faith.* [7]*If it is serving, let him serve; if it is teaching, let him teach;* [8]*if it is encouraging, let him encourage; if it is contributing to the needs of others, let him give generously; if it is leadership, let him govern diligently; if it is showing mercy, let him do it cheerfully.*

In discussing what might be called our relationship with ourselves, Paul writes that we must view ourselves soberly and then serve in the family of God in keeping with who he has really designed us to be. Our roles in the body are shown in terms of humility, function and gifts. Humility (v3) is a matter of seeing ourselves soberly—literally, "to be in one's right mind." (Who are we, *really?*) When we clearly see God and the blessings of the salvation he has given us, then we can look at ourselves in the right way. And when we see ourselves correctly we realize that we need to function together with others, not on our own.

"Function" (vv4-5) means that we have different roles in the body because we belong to the others in the body, and we need all of the different body functions in order to be healthy, as is the case with our physical bodies.

Gifts (vv6-8) are described to some degree, not to fully list nor explain all the gifts available in the body, but to demonstrate the view we are to have toward ourselves. Nearly all of these gifts, with the exception of prophesying, are what we call natural, or nonmiraculous.[1] They have been called "genetic" and "environmental" gifts. In other words, we are born with special talents or capabilities, and our environment has served to help develop them. All the gifts are to be used for the purpose of serving others and not for serving ourselves. The gifts of the whole body then *reveal* Christ. (Compare Colossians 2:9 with Ephesians 1:22-23— just as Christ revealed the fullness of *God*, the church reveals the fullness of *Christ!*) Therefore, leaving out part of the gifts diminishes our representation and manifestation of Jesus Christ.

We need to distinguish between gifts and responsibilities; they are not the same thing. For example, not all have the *gift* of financially contributing, but all still have the *responsibility* of financially contributing. Those who do have any particular gift serve as examples for the rest of us to help us grow in that area, to better carry out our responsibility. "Let him" use his gifts—this is a repeated idea here. We need to seek to use our own gifts, but we need to greatly encourage everyone else to use and develop their own gifts—without pushing them past the point of their own faith (v3). The issue is that God determines the gifts and roles for the good of the whole body. These roles have nothing to do with how important or valuable we are to God and to one another. To be even a doorkeeper in the house of God is an exalted privilege (Psalm 84:10).

Our Individual Spiritual Worth

However, it is easier to state the doorkeeper principle than it is to internalize it emotionally. Most of us struggle with the person we see in the mirror and often allow Satan, the great accuser, to win the day. We need to think through this whole issue in order to derail the devil. When it comes to understanding our gifts from God and the way that they are to be used in his family, many of us feel far too unimportant, insignificant and valueless. Asking ourselves a few questions might be a good way to get in touch with these feelings of inferiority. For example, how important is *your* role in the church? How important are *you* to God? Are these two questions related—does the answer to the second depend on the answer to the first? Keep your thinking cap on as you continue to read. How important is a one-week-old baby in the running of a household (helping with the chores, answering the phone, etc.) compared to the help that a twelve-year-old child might be able to give? How important is the one-week-old baby to the parents? (Is the baby less important than the twelve-year-old?)

Do you get the point? We often base our worth spiritually on how noticeable a role we have in the kingdom, and yet God simply does not view us that way. Our worth before God is not based on what we do, but on whose we are! Understanding roles in the church will make us feel far better about ourselves, each other, God and the kingdom in general. Let's jump into the study, raise our understanding in a number of areas, and see what blessings God has for us.

Our Celebration of Differences

Without question, we do have some challenges to deal with if we are to find the joy in Christ and his body that God so much desires for us. Among these challenges are the differences among disciples. We are all different from one another in many ways. Some of these differences pose no problem for us at all—in fact, we glory in them. Some of the differences in this category are racial, cultural, educational, age and socioeconomic differences.

We rejoice to be in a church in which prejudices have been dealt with to such a large degree, for it is a great testimony to a world in which each of these differences brings disunity and mistrust.

On the other hand, we sometimes have trouble with the differences between us in the spiritual realm. When others have talents that we do not have, or when they have successes that we do not have, it is easy to feel bad about ourselves, about them or about both! Frankly, some of us get so caught up in performance that we cannot perform effectively: our frustrations rule out faith, which in turn rules out effectiveness. Unless we learn to accept who we are, relax and enjoy our lives, our future in the kingdom is not a bright one. But God wants it to be, and he is able to make it bright—we simply must learn to cooperate with him.

For example, if all trees were the same, or all flowers, or all animals, or if anything else in nature were completely alike, God's creation would not be nearly as exciting and rewarding. And we would be disappointed! Would our Creator have taken such pains to provide the remarkable variety in his physical creation and then have planned for all of us to be just alike? Hardly! We have much to learn about rejoicing in our differences, do we not?

A specific spiritual challenge that we as disciples face is that of our differences in effectiveness in the mission of seeking and saving the lost. We all have the charge of accomplishing this tremendously important task. But are we to accomplish it in exactly the same way? For the most part, we tend to think that the approaches to being effective in evangelism must be the same for everyone. After all, does not the discipling process involve learning from another person and imitating them? While learning from others and imitating them are valid parts of growth, they are not rigid and mechanical principles. We learn and we imitate, but we are still ourselves, and the learning must fit into who we really are as human beings.

A key to accepting our differences is found in knowing what about us can and should be changed (as far as approach and method are concerned), and what about us is a continuing part of who we are as individuals. The way that we will be most effective is to have a disciple's heart. We need to learn as much as possible from whomever, trying everything that we can do to be effective.

But then, we need to also look for what seems to be the most natural, most effective way for us as individuals. Problems arise when we try to be square pegs in round holes—we become bland, unmotivated and even more ineffective.

These differences in us must be viewed in a manner that allows us to maintain a healthy view of ourselves. But how we view ourselves is more than having a worldly concern about our own self-esteem. If we do not have God's view of ourselves, then we will be neither healthy nor happy. However, we often base our view of self on the view others have of us (or that we *think* they have of us) instead of on the view that God really has.

In the kingdom, some views have not been the best, although the origin of these views is quite understandable. For example, in a church planting, the need for ministry staff people is pressing. Thus, much emphasis is understandably placed on going into the "full-time ministry," as we usually term it. The problem arises when a person who is not suited for the ministry, for any one of a number of valid reasons, begins to feel like a second-class citizen of the kingdom. Actually, the term "full-time ministry" contributes to the problem and leaves a misleading (non-Biblical) impression. All disciples have a ministry (2 Corinthians 5:18), and all disciples are to be full-time (living) sacrifices (Romans 12:1). Therefore, all disciples are in the full-time ministry in a real sense of the word! The accurate distinction is that some are church-supported and others are self-supported—but we are all full-time ministry people in a definite sense. Is this distinction simply a trivial matter of terminology? Or, is it much more than that, affecting the way we see ourselves and therefore, affecting our effectiveness for the Lord?

Another related misconception arises when a congregation is in the role of sending out many mission plantings. Those who are not chosen to be a part of a team, whether in or out of the church-supported ministry, also can struggle with feeling like second-class citizens. When a congregation has the role of sending out plantings, the leaders must emphasize the need for such efforts. However, such an emphasis must be done in a way that those who do not go still feel like a vital part of the team and in no way inferior! The answer to these difficulties is to cultivate a correct view of our value, based on sound Biblical principles. If we base

our significance on the type of role we have or on our performance, we are being worldly.

Our Collective Spiritual Worth

A related challenge is that of truly appreciating the strengths
of our fellow disciples. This challenge can be fully met only when
we have a right view of ourselves and our roles. When we feel
good about our differences, then we also appreciate one another's
strengths. For example, on a football team, a running back may
struggle with attitudes toward another running back who is vying
for his position, but he is totally fired-up about great talent on the
offensive line! On God's team, no one is vying for our positions,
because God has as many positions as he has disciples—a tailor-
made plan for every one of us! When we love the mission of
Christ and comprehend even a portion of the magnitude of the
task before us, another's effectiveness causes us to rejoice and
appreciate their God-given talents. When we see ourselves as God
does, we have peace rather than anxiety, and we are freed up to
appreciate the strengths of our brothers and sisters.

Excursus: A Challenge to Leaders

What do leaders need to learn from this passage?
First, they need to *delegate*. In Romans 12:7-8, Paul says
"let him" seven times. Leaders who do not delegate are
either very prideful, very insecure or both. No one leader
has all the gifts, nor does even a group of leaders—it
takes *every member* of the body to form the fullness of
Christ. Therefore, leaders need to look for and develop
gifts in others and then use them to the greatest extent.
Leaders need to take some risks in encouraging others to
discover their gifts and put them into practice. As a
leader, your way of doing something might work best or
most efficiently, but if you don't allow others to try their
ideas out, you will stunt their growth.

Further, leaders need to seek input regarding their
own lives and their leadership. Since no one leader has
all the gifts, he not only needs to learn the fine art of del-
egation, but the humble art of seeking help. Leaders are
surrounded by people whom they themselves disciple in

Christ, for the most part, making it necessary to figure out a way to obtain input from the grassroots level on a consistent basis. Leaders also need to seek input—honest *critique*—from the other leaders around them, especially regarding their public speaking and their leading of various types of meetings. Failure to seek such input of ideas and critique will limit the effectiveness of a leader and therefore will limit the health and reproduction of the body of Christ as a whole.

Our Different Evangelistic Gifts

What will help us as individual disciples apply verses 6-9 to our lives in a practical way? For one thing, we need to figure out what our gifts actually are. Thinking about what we do best and enjoy the most will help us get a better idea of just what our gifts may be. We need to ask those who know us best what they think our greatest strengths are. We should also take a look at our inabilities and come to terms with them. Some of them can change and should be worked on diligently in order to change. Others will likely never change significantly no matter what we do. If this seems the case to you and others who help you to evaluate, then figure out a way to cover these inabilities and focus on maximizing your strengths! Then you will be happier and more effective. Now is the time to take initiative, be creative and launch out to become who God made you to be.

As I cautionary note, we are not discussing substituting good deeds for evangelism in the case of any disciple. We are making the case that a person working within the areas of his or her strengths will be both happier and more fruitful. The same old approaches to ministry may seem safe and secure, but surely God would like to move our ministries more powerfully! Let *them* (do their thing) and let *him* (do his thing)!

What are some applications to specific practical areas in ministry? Certainly we cannot provide a comprehensive list of all the possibilities within the practical areas, but we do want to provide enough to illustrate the point and to prompt much more thought in this direction. Consider the area of music for example. An outstanding musician will be far more effective reaching out as a performer to other performers, or to those highly interested in his performance, than he will be at the local convenience store. This does not mean that he should not share at the convenience store (people there may have no other contact with disciples), but it does mean that he will be far more confident and effective sharing in his own element. Obviously, we all need to keep growing in our confidence in God to use us in any setting, but in our element, others will see us in a different way than they would in the streets, and they will respond differently as well.

Consider women who enjoy aerobics or crafts or any other area of interest to women in our society. When they are around non-Christian women in their areas of mutual interest, they will be much more confident and effective in reaching out to them. Again, I am not suggesting that we should stop sharing with people as we go, but that we should all focus on areas of outreach which capitalize on who we are as people. Personally, when I am happy with my lot in life, doing what I do best, then my sharing is more natural.

Consider the area of public service. Matthew 25:31-46 makes it obvious that Jesus is very concerned with how we treat people who are physically needy, sick or in prison. One of the sectors in the Boston church is involved in both a jail ministry and a food pantry. They are visiting prisoners and studying with them, and they are feeding hundreds of people in their community who need and appreciate the help. These ministries are making a very good impression on those being helped, and the community is taking notice and desiring to help out in ways as well. Ask yourself if the people in that community will be *more* open or *less* open to sharing from those who are serving like Jesus did and like he told us to do. Also ask yourself whether those doing the serving will be *more* likely or *less* likely to share about Jesus and their church.

Surely the answers to these questions are obvious. The serving Christians will be more excited to share their faith; the ones being served or watching the serving will be more open; and God will bless the efforts to imitate Jesus and his type of ministry with fruit! Before the advent of mass evangelistic methods (blitzing, the one-a-day challenge, street preaching, campaigns, etc.), churches among our movement still grew at good rates. How? Mostly in the way that we have just discussed.

I do not doubt that God led us to methods of evangelism which enable us to reach out to large numbers of people that we may not have reached in any other way. On the other hand, I am convinced that he never intended for these to become a substitute for more natural, lifestyle, relationship evangelism. Some of us are basically isolationists who dash out of our little comfort zones to invite one or two people to a Bible talk or church and then dash back in to our protected environments, feeling at least a little better about ourselves as disciples.

It is time to repent of our cowardice, take up our places in society as the light and the salt and the leaven, and start making disciples the way Jesus did—with all evangelistic approaches. But like him, we must seek the ones that work the best in our societies. God made us as very unique individuals, and he intends to use our uniqueness for the purpose of glorifying his name in a way that no one else can. We need to appreciate how he has made us and who he has made us, and then cooperate with him and the ones he has placed in our lives in order to become all that we are meant to be. Let's love God, one another and our own roles in the kingdom—whatever they may be at any given time.

Love for Others (Romans 12:9-21)

> [9]Love must be sincere. Hate what is evil; cling to what is good. [10]Be devoted to one another in brotherly love. Honor one another above yourselves. [11]Never be lacking in zeal, but keep your spiritual fervor, serving the Lord. [12]Be joyful in hope, patient in affliction, faithful in prayer. [13]Share with God's people who are in need. Practice hospitality.
>
> [14]Bless those who persecute you; bless and do not curse. [15]Rejoice with those who rejoice; mourn with those who mourn. [16]Live in harmony with one another. Do not be proud, but be willing to associate with people of low position. Do not be conceited.
>
> [17]Do not repay anyone evil for evil. Be careful to do what is right in the eyes of everybody. [18]If it is possible, as far as it depends on you, live at peace with everyone. [19]Do

not take revenge, my friends, but leave room for God's
wrath, for it is written: "It is mine to avenge; I will repay,"
says the Lord. ²⁰*On the contrary:*

> *"If your enemy is hungry, feed him;*
>   *if he is thirsty, give him something to drink.*
> *In doing this, you will heap burning coals on his head."*

²¹*Do not be overcome by evil, but overcome evil with good.*

Paul goes on to describe our relationship with other
Christians. This section is a practical application of John 13:35.
Love is described in a variety of ways in this section. It is to be
"sincere"—meaning genuine, without hypocrisy. A sincere person
is one who is real, not trying to hide himself under false pretenses.
This love honors others above self and is truly devoted to relationships within the body of Christ. One of the best ways to love
one another is to stay fired up, for enthusiasm spreads! (v11). The
love of disciples is measured in terms of joy, patience, prayerful-
ness and being hospitable (vv12-13).

Responding well to those who hurt us as individuals is a
deeper challenge of Christ-like love (v14). Love produces
harmony and the ability to identify with others, no matter what
they may be experiencing (vv15-16). The very mention of our relationship with our enemies (vv17-21) recognizes the truth that we
will have enemies (John 15:18-20). But how do we treat them? Do
not seek retaliation—let them win their "be ugly" contests! Do set
an absolutely pure example. Make peace your goal, not
"winning"—with *everyone*, even those who test your patience and
heart the most. (Who is this in your life?) Serve your enemies in
every possible way. Trust God with the outcome, for evil *is* weaker
than good. Keep smiling and do the loving thing, for God will
ultimately win!

Romans 12 is a very logical application of the doctrine of salvation by grace through faith. When we come into a saved relationship with God through Christ, we come at the same time into

a special relationship with his other children. His sons and daughters are now our brothers and sisters. Learning to love them deeply is our Father's goal for us (1 Peter 1:22), and it must be a lifetime endeavor. Loving God with our whole being and our neighbors as ourselves is no small challenge (Matthew 22:36-40). Interestingly, Paul in Romans 12 recognizes that our view of self is a significant factor in how we meet this challenge. His order of viewing relationship—God, self and others—makes perfect sense. May God enable us to deal decisively with our selfishness and to let our love for him and others flow evermore freely!

Note

1. Even prophesying could refer to a "nonmiraculous" activity when one considers that a prophet is primarily one who brings the word of God to bear on a situation. Prophets are "forth-tellers" more often than they are miraculous foretellers.

13

The Christian and the Government
Romans 13

"Submission" is a word that sounds restrictive and negative to most of us. An exception to that generalization might be in the case of those with a military background, but for the rest of us, it seems to go against human nature. We are not naturally submissive people. Even our children grow up having to be reined in from rebellious tendencies that seem to be a part of their gene pool. I once read a good book entitled *The God Players*, which candidly describes our human tendency to want to be the god of our own lives.[1] What a challenge—learning to think and live under the umbrella of authority. We begin with God's authority and continue with the other authorities he has ordained in our lives. No doubt submission is a key ingredient of Christianity, and one of the more challenging.

Disciples are to be submissive in a number of different areas: to Christ (Ephesians 5:24); to one another (Ephesians 5:21); to leaders in the church (Hebrews 13:17); to masters, or by modern application, to employers (Ephesians 6:5-9); wives to husbands (Ephesians 5:22-24); children to parents (Ephesians 6:1-4); and citizens to leaders in the government (Romans 13:1-7).

Many look at voluntary submission as a sign of weakness, but God sees it as a sign of strength. The difficulty of embracing submission even intellectually, to say nothing of emotionally, shows that it is not for the weak. In Romans 13, we have three primary areas of submission to discuss: to government (vv1-7), to one another in love (vv8-10) and to righteous living (vv11-14).

Submission to Government (Romans 13:1-7)

> [13:1]*Everyone must submit himself to the governing authorities, for there is no authority except that which God has established. The authorities that exist have been established by God. [2]Consequently, he who rebels against the authority is rebelling against what God has instituted, and those who do so will bring judgment on themselves. [3]For rulers hold no terror for those who do right, but for those who do wrong. Do you want to be free from fear of the one in authority? Then do what is right and he will commend you. [4]For he is God's servant to do you good. But if you do wrong, be afraid, for he does not bear the sword for nothing. He is God's servant, an agent of wrath to bring punishment on the wrongdoer. [5]Therefore, it is necessary to submit to the authorities, not only because of possible punishment but also because of conscience.*
>
> [6]*This is also why you pay taxes, for the authorities are God's servants, who give their full time to governing. [7]Give everyone what you owe him: If you owe taxes, pay taxes; if revenue, then revenue; if respect, then respect; if honor, then honor.*

God commands submission to government, as Paul writes in verses 1-7—even with Nero, a violent persecutor of the church in power at the time. Paul views submission as a reasonable response to the governmental authorities God has established. Of course, God established the *principle* of national governments, without regard to the specific *type* of government (vv1-2). For example, those of us raised in democratic societies are prone to think that only this type of government is really approved by God, but democracy was not the prevailing type when Romans was written, nor has it been the most prevalent throughout history. I am grateful to live under a government that allows an amazing level of freedom, but God's mission on earth does not succeed or fail because of who rules and how. If God was able to evangelize the world under an autocrat in the first century, he can do it today under whatever governmental forms hold sway. God rules the nations!

God uses the governments as his agents to administer justice (Romans 13:1-5). Hence, we are to pray for the leaders of government, so that we might have peace, which makes the spreading of the gospel much easier (1 Timothy 2:1-4). Furthermore, rulers protect society by punishing wrongdoers and rewarding those who do good (vv3-4). Notice "bear the sword" in verse 4, which seems to be a reference to capital punishment. In many countries today, discussing this topic produces controversy. Certainly the controversy is understandable, especially in America where the rich often find a way to avoid capital punishment and those without substantial financial means are the ones most often executed. Add to this the fact that the minority races most often fit in that latter category, and the discussion becomes even more emotional.

Capital Punishment in the Old Testament

Regardless of what we feel about capital punishment, the Bible must determine our ultimate conclusions as disciples. We know for sure, at the outset, that God approved of many kinds of killing in the Old Testament, including capital punishment, under the legislation he inspired. For example a whole host of sins and crimes elicited the death penalty in the Mosaic Law.[2] Several modes of carrying out the death penalty are mentioned in the Old Testament, including burning (Genesis 38:24, Leviticus 20:14, 21:9), stoning (Leviticus 20:2, 27; 24:14; Numbers 14:10; 15:33-36), hanging (Deuteronomy 21:22-23, Joshua 8:29) and death by the sword (Exodus 32:27-28; 1 Kings 2:25, 34, 46).

At times, the executions were carried out by the authorities, as would be expected, but at other times, by the witnesses of a crime (Deuteronomy 13:6-9, 17:7). At still other times, executions were performed by the people as a whole (Numbers 15:35-36, Deuteronomy 13:9). In no instance was capital punishment to be inflicted on the testimony of less than two witnesses (Numbers 35:30; Deuteronomy 17:6, 19:15). What are we to make of all of this? Only that God believes in capital punishment and commanded its practice on a fairly broad basis in the OT period.[3]

Capital Punishment in the New Testament

As we study the teaching of the New Testament about capital punishment, we must dig a bit deeper. The heretic Marcion dug in the wrong direction, concluding that the God of the Old Testament (the Father) was harsh, while the God of the New Testament (Jesus) was full of grace. This solves no problems, for Jesus as the eternal *Logos* (the eternal Word in John 1:1) was with the Father from the beginning. Whatever the Father did in the Old Testament, Jesus did. Whatever Jesus does now, the Father does with him (John 10:30). "Jesus Christ is the same yesterday and today and forever" (Hebrews 13:8), and so is the Father. God is God and cannot be otherwise. Therefore, Marcion's "god" was not the God of Scripture.

To begin our consideration of the NT teaching on the subject, Romans 13:4 clearly indicates the legitimacy of capital punishment. It might be argued (though it is not my persuasion) that, like polygamy in the Old Testament and slavery in both the Old Testament and the New Testament, God allowed a practice that he knew would eventually be largely phased out by his deeper principles to the contrary. But even now one cannot be dogmatic in opposition to any of these three practices, however unnatural and distasteful they may be to our modern thinking. Both polygamy and slavery have again become issues in some societies into which the gospel is being sent—calling for wisdom, rather than rigid opinions, on the part of church leaders.

In his book, *Q & A: Answers to Bible Questions You Have Asked*, Douglas Jacoby makes the point that Romans 13 answers the question about the right of a state to enforce capital punishment, but when we ask if a disciple should ever be in the role of taking the life of another person, we are asking a different question. In the next chapter of Romans Paul will show us that we sin whenever we go against our own conscience. Therefore, a disciple might conclude that the state has the right to carry out capital punishment but he would not be able to participate in its implementation.[4]

As a citizen of a country, we have some governmental rights that we cannot, as disciples, exercise. I assumedly have the legal *right* to view pornography, commit immorality and drink alcohol to excess. But as a disciple, my higher allegiance to God's spiritual laws supersede what government allows. In other words, what the government does or allows is not the end of the matter for me personally as a disciple.

Acting As an Agent of the State

The more sensitive issue is the possibility of a Christian acting in this capacity as an agent of the state. In other words, can a disciple of Jesus destroy life as a member of the military or other branch of law enforcement? I see some differences between the two. Those with whom law enforcement officers deal are supposed criminals, while those in another country's military force may be innocent pawns of their own government.

As this book goes to press, the military issue now looms very large in our minds following the heinous terrorist attacks against New York City and Washington D.C. on September 11, 2001. It did not take long for our nation's utter shock and disbelief to become anger and the desire for vengeance. Many disciples, if they are honest, have struggled with the same attitudes. What answers does the Bible offer on this emotionally charged issue?

In the Old Testament, wars were commonplace for the Israelite nation. However, we must remember that civil and religious laws were intertwined for them, since they were the nation of God—a theocracy. Also, they most often went into battle after being directed to do so by God. In the New Testament, there is a separation of church and state, which ushers in some different principles. While we are citizens of two kingdoms at once, our higher calling is to the kingdom of God. Certainly we are to be under the authority of our government, but only as long as it does not violate the authority of God (see Acts 4:18-20, 5:27-29). The Old Testament predicted this difference in passages like Isaiah 2:1-4, in which the prophet said that in the new kingdom "they will beat their swords into plowshares and their spears into pruning hooks. Nation will not take up sword against nation, nor will they train for war anymore" (v4).

Jesus foretold the destruction of Jerusalem that occurred in 70 AD and warned his disciples to flee, rather than to fight, when it happened (Luke 21:20-21). Jesus told Pilate that the kingdom he was bringing was not of this world and had it been, then his servants would have fought (John 18:36). Read Matthew 5:38-48 and Romans 12:17-21 carefully. Here we learn that when we are persecuted for our spiritual convictions, clearly we cannot fight fire with fire. We are to love our spiritual enemies, not hate them. God hates those who love violence (Psalm 11:4-7). Vengeance belongs to God (Romans 12:19), and we need to trust him with it— whether in this life or on Judgment Day.

Therefore, what the government does, it does. Governments are agents of God to deliver justice, but this does not automatically grant a disciple the right to participate in that process. My participation or lack thereof is another matter, since my highest allegiance is to God's law.

The question of whether a Christian can engage in military service has been an issue with which I have wrestled since I was a teenager. At age eighteen, I had to register with the Selective Service System (a.k.a. the draft). Then I had to make a choice about my willingness to bear arms and possibly take another's life. We have many brothers in different countries who are required to be in the military. We also have police officers and other similar agents of the state who are converted while serving in these capacities. What should their position be about these matters as new disciples?

My understanding is that the early church solved this dilemma by allowing those converted to remain in military or law enforcement roles until they could get out of them gracefully, but disciples did not accept such roles after conversion. At age eighteen, in an unusual move for people in that cultural setting, I registered for the draft as a conscientious objector, meaning that I would be willing to serve in the military in a capacity that did not require bearing arms. Although my religious commitment was severely limited in general at that point of my life, I did have convictions in this area. These convictions have remained the same in the forty years since, although I do think the complexity of the subject makes it a personal matter of conscience. When my son was concerned about the possibility of the draft being resumed during the Gulf War, I shared my thoughts with him and then encouraged him to talk to some of my spiritually mature friends on both sides of the issue.

In light of the recent calamitous events in America, the subject is no longer an intellectual issue—it is a very practical one. Even the fact that we have now planted churches in all major nations of the earth demands that we proceed with Biblical caution and not be carried away by emotions. I do not intend to shoot at someone on the other side who might be a brother in Christ, and I am thankful that the American government allows young men and women this choice. Other governments may not, and no matter what the country, we must struggle with our own consciences and convictions. As with all difficult subjects, I respect your right to come to a different conclusion than I have come to.

Even though I am settled in my conclusion, the most difficult aspect of it comes by recognizing that two principles can be in conflict, thus prompting a choice between them. For example, love for God supersedes love for family, and we may have to choose him over them (Matthew 10:34-37). Similarly, love for family supersedes love for enemies, and we may have to choose the former over the latter.

What would you do if an intruder broke into your home and threatened the safety of your family? Would you use force, perhaps killing the intruder in the process? If you answered, "Possibly" or "Probably," you assumedly would answer the same way if that intruder was a member of an enemy military group. Then, some would argue, why would you not go abroad as a member of our military forces and protect your family before the enemy made it to your front doorstep? Hopefully you can see that this topic is not easy for any of us. I am glad that God promised that we will not be tempted with anything beyond what we can bear and that he will provide the way to endure trials (1 Corinthians 10:13). Let's study the subject, ask counsel of many advisors, make personal decisions about how we are going to deal with it, and then extend grace to those who come out on the other side of the issue.

Submission to Laws and Taxes

Paul continues in Romans 13:5 with a comment about conscience in a different setting. He shows that the violation of the laws of the land violates our consciences, and he shows that our submission to government is to be seen in terms of our acceptance of the responsibility to pay taxes and to respect officials (vv6-7). Both of these should be done in faith by disciples. In Titus 3:1-2, he warns Christians about ever speaking evil of such officials, and

1 Timothy 2:1-2 enjoins us to always pray for them. Certainly we must balance these passages with the principle found in Acts 5:29 which demands that we obey God when his laws are different from man's. But even then, our attitudes must remain submissive, never even bordering on the rebellious.

Submission to One Another (Romans 13:8-10)

> [8]*Let no debt remain outstanding, except the continuing debt to love one another, for he who loves his fellowman has fulfilled the law. [9]The commandments, "Do not commit adultery," "Do not murder," "Do not steal," "Do not covet," and whatever other commandment there may be, are summed up in this one rule: "Love your neighbor as yourself." [10]Love does no harm to its neighbor. Therefore love is the fulfillment of the law.*

Submission to each other must be done in love. Paul also writes that we should not build up worldly debts, and although not the main focus here, this subject is definitely worth discussing. We in America are living in a debt-ridden society, brought on by the presence of materialistic hearts and the absence of discipline and self-control. Many become disciples with the consequences of such sins hanging around their necks like a millstone. What we did as non-Christians, we did, but as disciples, we must get much advice and bring our finances under the submission of Jesus Christ.

A brother whom I studied with many years ago came into the kingdom with a small, struggling business. He found himself as a young, single disciple with a failed business and a debt of more than $100,000. He refused to declare bankruptcy and determined to pay back every cent of the debt. In the next five years, he did exactly that, while giving financially to the church and even finding a wife! We need more convictions about such matters. Christians who are careless and undisciplined in finances (which is to say, unrighteous) usually cause other Christians and non-Christians to struggle and perhaps stumble. Spiritual light draws people to Christ; spiritual darkness—including financial unrighteousness—repulses and repels. If your conscience is convicted upon reading this, get open, get input and repent. "Let no debt remain outstanding" without a plan to pay it off.

However important financial responsibility may be, the main focus of this passage is on the need to *stay* in debt—the debt of love to the brothers. Love fulfills all the "one another" commands of the New Testament. Love for God is our primary motivation to serve him, and love for others is our highest obligation in human relationships (Matthew 22:36-40). Read through 1 Corinthians 13:4-7 and put Jesus' name in place of the word "love." Do the same with your name. How did you feel about the comparison? How keenly do you feel the debt to love others more than self? It is the heart of discipleship.

Submission to Righteous Living (Romans 13:11-14)

> *[11]And do this, understanding the present time. The hour has come for you to wake up from your slumber, because our salvation is nearer now than when we first believed. [12]The night is nearly over; the day is almost here. So let us put aside the deeds of darkness and put on the armor of light. [13]Let us behave decently, as in the daytime, not in orgies and drunkenness, not in sexual immorality and debauchery, not in dissension and jealousy. [14]Rather, clothe yourselves with the Lord Jesus Christ, and do not think about how to gratify the desires of the sinful nature.*

Submission to righteous living is discussed next (vv11-14). Paul says, "Wake up!" You are closer to death and judgment than ever before. What causes us to "slumber," to lose our "edge," to lose our "first love"? (Revelation 2:4). What helps us to wake up? "Put aside" and "put on" are vital analogies for staying in the paths of righteousness. Getting sin out of our lives is an ever-present need. However, if we do not put righteousness in its place, we will be worse off than in the beginning (see Matthew 12:43-45). Being "clothed" with Christ starts at baptism (Galatians 3:27), but we see from Romans 13:14 that it must continue daily. The sins of verse 13 are blatant, but they often do not start that way. When we lose focus, we gradually drift into more and more sins (Hebrews 2:1). Satan is patient. He is willing to bide his time and gradually lull us into spiritual sleep. Hence, *wake up*! Put aside and put on!

Romans 13 provides us with direction about some of the more significant issues relating to the topic of submission. Submission is neither easy nor optional. It is all about Biblical faith in action, for submission with proper attitudes is possible only when we believe God has both ordained it and will work through it in our lives. Romans is a book about faith, from beginning to end, and chapter 13 is no exception. Submitting to governmental authorities, to the needs of other disciples and to righteous living takes a deep faith in the God who authored it all. May he help us to grow in this highly essential Christian grace, for it demonstrates faith in a way that settles our hearts and draws the hearts of others to their Maker!

Notes

1. Editor's note: This book is out of print, but you may be able to find a used copy by searching on the World Wide Web.

2. Murder (Genesis 9:5-6; Numbers 35:16-21, 30-33; Deuteronomy 17:6), adultery (Leviticus 20:10, Deuteronomy 22:24), incest (Leviticus 20:11-12, 14), bestiality (Exodus 22:19, Leviticus 20:15-16), sodomy (Leviticus 18:22, 20:13), lack of virginity discovered on the wedding night (Deuteronomy 22:21-24), rape of an engaged virgin (Deuteronomy 22:25), kidnapping (Exodus 21:16, Deuteronomy 24:7), immorality of a priest's daughter (Leviticus 21:9), witchcraft (Exodus 22:18), offering human sacrifice (Leviticus 20:2-5), striking or cursing father or mother (Exodus 21:15, 17; Leviticus 20:9), flagrant disobedience to parents (Deuteronomy 21:18-21), blasphemy (Leviticus 24:11-16, 23), desecration of the Sabbath (Exodus 35:2, Numbers 15:32-36), false prophesying (Deuteronomy 13:1-10), sacrificing to false gods (Exodus 22:20), refusing to abide by the decision of the court (Deuteronomy 17:12) and treason (1 Kings 2:12-46; Esther 2:21-23).

3. In an interestingly related vein, Douglas Jacoby, in his book *Q & A: Answers to Bible Questions You Have Asked* (Billerica, Mass.: Discipleship Publications International, 2001), pages 162-193, spoke about the punishment of the wicked in eternity. In the essay entitled "Reexamining the Biblical Doctrine of Hell" under the section "Heaven and Hell—Terminal Punishment," he wrote this: "The terminal view is simply that after a period of torment ('corporal punishment') suited to the individual, God destroys him or her ('capital punishment')." Douglas admits that his terminal view has not been the traditional view in our movement and might not be the view held by the majority even now. However, if it is true (and I personally am persuaded that it is),

capital punishment, even of an everlasting nature, would need to be seen as godly and righteous. In that sense, God's own practice would have to influence what we think about what he ordained governmental authorities to practice.

4. Douglas Jacoby, *Q & A: Answers to Bible Questions You Have Asked* (Billerica, Mass.: Discipleship Publications International, 2001) 132-133.

14

Tolerance in Handling Our Differences
Romans 14

As the family of God, we must learn how to deal with family differences, and chapter 14 in Romans makes it perfectly clear that there is room in the kingdom for differences. This thought may disturb some with an idealistic view of unity, but humans must sort this reality out in all our relationships, from the job setting to the home. No husband and wife agree on everything. No set of parents and children agree on everything—especially when those children become teens! The unity of a home or a church is not threatened by some differences of opinion as long as they are dealt with in a spiritual way.

We have a little plaque in our home that reads: "The goal of marriage is not to think alike, but to think together." Well said. If two people agree on everything, one of them is absolutely unnecessary in decision making. One of the great benefits of our differences is that we can get a bigger picture of issues by seeing them from different perspectives. However, having said that, let me hasten to say that forging unity amidst those differences is sometimes fraught with difficulty, whether in our little families or in God's big family. For this reason, Paul was guided by the Holy Spirit to pen this section of Romans. We simply must learn to keep our hearts together in spite of differences—and the tensions they can cause.

Opinion—or Not? (Romans 14:1-12)

14:1Accept him whose faith is weak, without passing judgment on disputable matters. 2One man's faith allows him to eat everything, but another man, whose faith is weak, eats only vegetables. ³*The man who eats everything must not look down on him who does not, and the man who does not eat everything must not condemn the man who does, for God has accepted him.* ⁴*Who are you to judge someone else's servant? To his own master he stands or falls. And he will stand, for the Lord is able to make him stand.*

⁵*One man considers one day more sacred than another; another man considers every day alike. Each one should be fully convinced in his own mind.* ⁶*He who regards one day as special, does so to the Lord. He who eats meat, eats to the Lord, for he gives thanks to God; and he who abstains, does so to the Lord and gives thanks to God.* ⁷*For none of us lives to himself alone and none of us dies to himself alone.* ⁸*If we live, we live to the Lord; and if we die, we die to the Lord. So, whether we live or die, we belong to the Lord.*

⁹*For this very reason, Christ died and returned to life so that he might be the Lord of both the dead and the living.* ¹⁰*You, then, why do you judge your brother? Or why do you look down on your brother? For we will all stand before God's judgment seat.*

¹¹*It is written:*

> *"'As surely as I live,' says the Lord,*
> *'every knee will bow before me;*
>   *every tongue will confess to God.'"*

¹²*So then, each of us will give an account of himself to God.*

As we begin to examine the gist of Paul's argument, it is essential to understand the first century background out of which the differences arose. Jews and Gentiles in the early church had very different backgrounds in spiritual and moral areas. Once in the kingdom, differences of opinion and conscience were a source of much tension between the two groups. Specifically, some had a conscience issue about eating meat that may have been sacrificed to an idol and later sold in a meat market. Take the time to read 1 Corinthians 8 now, because Paul makes this point very clearly there. Also, some felt a special attraction toward certain holy days from their past. In essence, Paul shows that while these things are allowed, they cannot be bound on others. He urges us to be understanding of others' differences while careful of our own consciences and examples.

The differences here are in the realm of opinion, to be sure, but how can you tell if an area is an opinion area? Good question, but not an easy one. When good brothers who love God and his word have consistent differences on a given subject, we had better guard ourselves from having dogmatic attitudes. To one, a given issue may seem quite clear, but the issue may be not at all clear to another. In such areas, abide by your own personal conscience, but avoid dogmatism. What are such areas for us today? Drinking alcohol, dancing, dress, and watching movies with certain ratings, to name a few, would fall into our category of opinion areas.

Since Paul discusses the observation of holy days (holidays), the question naturally arises about the legitimacy of continuing to observe special days from our former religions. With such issues, we may not be comparing apples with apples. Jewish special days had been ordained by God, but with the advent of the new covenant of Christ, they were superseded. However, from passages like Acts 21, it is obvious that God allowed the Jewish Christians a transition period, in which they were allowed to remain fairly Jewish in practice, although only as a matter of custom, not of faith. To illustrate, Paul circumcised Timothy as an expedient (Acts 16:1-3), but rigorously refused to circumcise Titus to please the Judaizing teachers in Antioch (Galatians 2:3). A transitional period was apparently allowed by God, but according to Hebrews 8:13, the old covenant was said to be obsolete, aging and about to pass away. Thus, we must be careful in comparing our observance of holy days that were totally man-made to those that were originally God ordained.

What does Paul make of the difference between those with strong and weak faith? A person with strong faith can participate, while the person with weak faith cannot, without violating his conscience. Strength of faith in one area does not necessarily correspond to strong or weak faith in other areas. In other words, this person of strong faith regarding the eating of meats and observance of special days may have weak faith in evangelism and vice versa. Whether weak or strong, there is simply no room in the kingdom for maintaining judgmental attitudes (vv9-12). Narrow-mindedness and self-righteousness are sins of the Pharisees with which Jesus had zero tolerance, for they always produce disunity. True righteousness cannot be legislated by rules and regulations. Once we start down this legalistic path to spirituality, there will be no end to it—at least, not a good end!

On the other hand, guidelines are often needed. Before I became a part of the discipling movement, I heard criticism about so-called "dating rules." As parents, these guidelines sounded like a wonderful idea to Theresa and me, and they proved to be exactly that for our children. They dated righteously and ended up with incredible mates—absolutely perfect for them! But discerning the difference between legalistic rules and spiritual guidelines is so important for us. It is easier to legislate than it is to teach spiritual discernment.

In chapter 14, as Paul addresses these issues involving opinion and faith, one thing is perfectly clear: We must avoid divisions in heart over opinion issues. Lessons regarding authority are very relevant to this discussion. There are essentially three areas to consider in the use of leadership authority. One, when God's word specifically states something, there can be no doubt about the authority to enforce it. Two, recognized leaders of a congregation—the leadership group—can determine policies for the church which help everyone to carry out God's general commands (learning the Bible, evangelizing, etc.). Hebrews 13:17 refers to these leaders and this procedure of setting directions. Three, the giving of advice is the area that most demands wisdom of application. This is such a vital area for the disciple's life that I suggest that you take the time to read either chapter 11 in *Discipling* or chapter 10 in *The Power of Discipling*[1] for much more detail about the godly practice of giving and receiving advice before proceeding further.

Consider Others Better Than Yourselves (Romans 14:13-23)

> [13]*Therefore let us stop passing judgment on one another. Instead, make up your mind not to put any stumbling block or obstacle in your brother's way. *[14]*As one who is in the Lord Jesus, I am fully convinced that no food*

is unclean in itself. But if anyone regards something as unclean, then for him it is unclean. [15]If your brother is distressed because of what you eat, you are no longer acting in love. Do not by your eating destroy your brother for whom Christ died. [16]Do not allow what you consider good to be spoken of as evil. [17]For the kingdom of God is not a matter of eating and drinking, but of righteousness, peace and joy in the Holy Spirit, [18]because anyone who serves Christ in this way is pleasing to God and approved by men.

[19]Let us therefore make every effort to do what leads to peace and to mutual edification. [20]Do not destroy the work of God for the sake of food. All food is clean, but it is wrong for a man to eat anything that causes someone else to stumble. [21]It is better not to eat meat or drink wine or to do anything else that will cause your brother to fall.

[22]So whatever you believe about these things keep between yourself and God. Blessed is the man who does not condemn himself by what he approves. [23]But the man who has doubts is condemned if he eats, because his eating is not from faith; and everything that does not come from faith is sin.

Paul goes on in Romans 14:13-23 to show that there is no room in the kingdom for behavior that destroys or injures the faith of another. Correct and incorrect applications of this passage have often been made. An incorrect application may come through a misunderstanding of what it means to cause someone to stumble. This does not mean that someone just does not like your choices and grumbles about them. Jesus caused many people to grumble by violating their traditions, but he was most careful not to cause a weak person to stumble.

> A bruised reed he will not break,
>   and a smoldering wick he will not snuff out,
> till he leads justice to victory. (Matthew 12:20)

In the context of Romans 14, the one caused to stumble was a young Christian with an untrained conscience in certain areas, not an older, cranky legalist. (Again, consider how Jesus handled each type of person as he came across them in his ministry.) The way a weak brother was caused to stumble was by following the example of another in doing something that the weak brother's conscience would not allow. Reread all of 1 Corinthians 8 for a carefully worded explanation of this principle.

The "strong" must be spiritual. They must not insist on exercising their liberty at the expense of another. Ask yourself, weak or strong, how important your liberty is to you anyway (v17). We must all be willing to forfeit our rights in order to help younger Christians. Consider Paul's example in 1 Corinthians 9, in which he shares that he had given up his rights to some very significant things, such as financial support by the church and having a wife. In light of his example, we should hang our heads in shame when we get so impassioned about the exercise of our so-called rights. We are slaves of Jesus Christ. Slaves do not have rights, only privileges. The first step in coming to Jesus is self-denial, and this is the last step that our selfish natures want to take. Hence, we are faced with the absolute necessity of denying our self-promoting natural tendencies.

Paul continues in Romans 14:22-23 with a warning against violating our own consciences. Consciences can be changed by retraining (and often should be), but they should not be violated during the process. How about you? In what areas of conscience do you walk too close to the line? An honest evaluation of these matters is always helpful.

Whatever else may be said about Romans 14, God put the passage in the Bible to help us to maintain unity in the midst of our differences. Keep your minds and hearts open when dealing with difficult opinion issues, and do not be too quick to declare that such issues are a matter of faith rather than opinion. Know this for sure: when your emotions get hooked during such discussions, Satan is entering your heart.

My own heart and character were marked significantly by being raised in a religious group that did not practice the principles of Romans 14. Each person thought, as the old saying goes, that he had the truth in a wee, small box—and that he had the key to the lock! If we understand that the gospel is the message of grace freely received through faith, God will deliver us from that kind of unloving, disunifying legalism. May he grant that our differences be few and our agreements be many as we keep our purpose and mission clear. A preacher supposedly said something to this effect more than a century ago: "Remember that while we may disagree in the *hundredths*, we agree in the *thousands*." Amen to that!

Our purpose is eternal—to glorify God with all our being in all that we do. Our mission is to pour out our lives during our brief sojourn on planet Earth to seek and to save the lost, winning as many as possible. When our minds and hearts are governed by these two principles, Romans 14 will prove to be a map for solutions, not a playground for contention. May the Lord Jesus himself help us deal quickly and effectively with minor issues, as we hold heart and soul to the major truths!

Note

1. Gordon Ferguson, *Discipling—God's Plan to Train and Transform His People* (Billerica, Mass.: Discipleship Publications International, 1997) 162-170, and *The Power of Discipling* (Billerica, Mass.: Discipleship Publications International, 2001) 145-152.

15

One Heart and One Goal
Romans 15

Romans 15 is simply a continuation of Romans 14, showing that both strong and weak are in one family, and they need to act like it. It is not enough simply to resign ourselves to having opinion differences. It is not acceptable to cover our inner bitterness with a casual, "Oh, that's just the way she is." Differences have a way of decreasing our appreciation for each other and destroying love. We are prideful enough to be put off by those who do not accept our view of things. Selfishness causes us take things personally that are not intended to be personal. For example, even when studying the Bible with others, we can emotionally be much more disturbed by their rejection of *our* presentation of truth than by their rejection of the Truth-Giver. And if that happens when presenting Biblical truth, how much more can we become petty and unloving when our mere personal opinions are not readily accepted. No wonder Paul continues his discourse on the weak and the strong as he pleads with us to be a loving family.

Love Like Jesus' (Romans 15:1-7)

15:1 We who are strong ought to bear with the failings of the weak and not to please ourselves. 2 Each of us should please his neighbor for his good, to build him up. 3 For even Christ did not please himself but, as it is written: "The insults of those who insult you have fallen on me." 4 For everything that was written in the past was written to teach us, so that through endurance and the encouragement of the Scriptures we might have hope.

5 May the God who gives endurance and encouragement give you a spirit of unity among yourselves as you

> *follow Christ Jesus, ⁶so that with one heart and mouth you*
> *may glorify the God and Father of our Lord Jesus Christ.*
> *⁷Accept one another, then, just as Christ accepted you,*
> *in order to bring praise to God.*

Paul builds on what he said about the relationship between those with strong consciences in opinion areas and those with weaker consciences. He had written that Christians should not look down on others or condemn them (Romans 14:1-12), nor should they allow their influence to negatively affect the conduct of other disciples (14:13-23). In Romans 15 he gives a third principle to observe when a believer is dealing with his fellow Christians: He is to follow the example of the Lord Jesus Christ. Jesus did not please himself (v3), and since we are to follow him (v5), we must accept one another as we have already been accepted by Jesus (v7).

Bearing with the weak is a part of everyday life, especially in a physical family. Just ask any parent about that. Babies may be little bundles of joy from heaven, but they are incredibly weak. Their every need must be met by the parents, who normally are delighted to do so. We do not expect babies to contribute much to the family except noise and odors! Yet, we love them and want to take care of them. Adults who otherwise may be self-centered are called to sacrifice when they become parents, and they are the better for it. Their characters deepen, and they begin to understand the principle of self-denial in a much clearer way.

Husbands are directed to be sensitive with their wives, who are said to be the weaker partners (in some sense but certainly not in most senses—1 Peter 3:7). We men tend to be self-sufficient and self-centered, but taking a wife necessitates our learning the fine art of sensitivity and sacrifice. Getting married is a wonderful way to have our characters refined, and we are blessed by taking on the responsibilities of this unique covenant of sharing. Also, older siblings understand that the younger children in the family are weaker and must be protected. Some of our closest emotional relationships are forged when we are thus caring for our younger, and therefore weaker, physical brothers and sisters. We take pride in performing this role of being big sister or big brother. The sacrifices we make help us feel more needed and more valuable.

Why do we have problems applying these same principles in a spiritual family? And we often do. It has to be that we do not love at nearly the same depth. Jesus made clear that to make sacrifices for the gospel ensured multiple blessings, including family relationships in the church (Mark 10:29-30). Do we understand and appreciate these relationships?

I remember growing up in a family that had a strong sense of family identity (at least on my father's side). It meant something to be a Ferguson, for Fergusons stuck together. I was so much a part of this heritage that I could not have imagined feeling closer to nonrelatives than to my grandparents, uncles and aunts. I had especially close relationships with my father's mother and his two younger brothers when I was growing up. They were my friends and my heroes. I idolized them. But what I felt for them does not compare to what I feel now for hundreds of brothers and sisters in Christ. Is this the way you feel? Why would we feel closer to those who are not going to be in eternity with us than to those who are? Our perspectives may need some adjustments on these things; the ones to whom Paul originally wrote definitely needed adjustments in their thinking.

Carrying one another's burdens is a major way in which we fulfill the law of Christ (Galatians 6:2). His law is a law of love, aimed at helping us to love God with our whole being and to love our neighbors as ourselves (Matthew 22:36-40). As Paul said earlier in Romans, "Let no debt remain outstanding, except the continuing debt to love one another, for he who loves his fellowman has fulfilled the law" (Romans 13:8). The high-water mark of loving is when we love the unlovely. Jesus loved us and died for us while we were still his enemies, in rebellion against heaven by our sins. Remember what he said in Matthew 5:46: "If you love those who love you, what reward will you get? Are not even the tax collectors doing that?"

In our physical families, we learn to love the weak; we must do the same in God's family. We not only need to love the weak— we need to see our *need* for the weak. Paul so stated in 1 Corinthians 12:22: "On the contrary, those parts of the body that seem to be weaker are indispensable." Is that how we feel about the weak in our fellowship? Do we enjoy serving them, knowing that they cannot or will not pay us back? Or are they a bother to us? The inherent differences between the strong and the weak in the first century church were of a magnitude that Paul used much ink in correcting their views of each other. We are not such spiritual giants that we have escaped the same challenges.

Let us spend some good time thinking about who the weak are among us and start serving them in a serious way. We are often so focused on our agendas that we do not even notice them. Like the priest and the Levite in Luke 10, we pass right by the weak, time and time again, without really even seeing them (vv30-37). God help us to open our eyes and hearts and to become those Good Samaritans of our day!

On the other hand, if you would consider yourself one of the weak, resolve that you will not stay that way. We will always have those who are weak. The church will never be lacking at this point, but it is God's will for everyone who is weak to seek to become strong. No one will be more prepared to help weak Christians than a formerly weak Christian who has grown and overcomes challenges.

Love and Trust Destroy Prejudice (Romans 15:8-19)

> [8]For I tell you that Christ has become a servant of the Jews on behalf of God's truth, to confirm the promises made to the patriarchs [9]so that the Gentiles may glorify God for his mercy, as it is written:
>
> > "Therefore I will praise you among the Gentiles;
> > I will sing hymns to your name."
>
> [10]Again, it says,
>
> > "Rejoice, O Gentiles, with his people."
>
> [11]And again,
>
> > "Praise the Lord, all you Gentiles,
> > and sing praises to him, all you peoples."

¹²And again, Isaiah says,

> "The Root of Jesse will spring up,
>   one who will arise to rule over the nations;
> the Gentiles will hope in him."

¹³May the God of hope fill you with all joy and peace as you trust in him, so that you may overflow with hope by the power of the Holy Spirit.

¹⁴I myself am convinced, my brothers, that you yourselves are full of goodness, complete in knowledge and competent to instruct one another. ¹⁵I have written you quite boldly on some points, as if to remind you of them again, because of the grace God gave me ¹⁶to be a minister of Christ Jesus to the Gentiles with the priestly duty of proclaiming the gospel of God, so that the Gentiles might become an offering acceptable to God, sanctified by the Holy Spirit.

¹⁷Therefore I glory in Christ Jesus in my service to God. ¹⁸I will not venture to speak of anything except what Christ has accomplished through me in leading the Gentiles to obey God by what I have said and done—¹⁹by the power of signs and miracles, through the power of the Spirit. So from Jerusalem all the way around to Illyricum, I have fully proclaimed the gospel of Christ.

In this section, Paul focuses on the Gentiles' inclusion in the family of God. Not surprisingly, the strong and the weak likely tended to be differentiated along racial lines: Jew and Gentile. Why else would Paul spend the time with this focus on showing that Gentiles were a part of God's plan from the beginning? It is difficult in our modern setting to understand the deep rift between these two groups that had existed for centuries, producing suspicion, distrust, dislike and even hatred. (Perhaps the ongoing strife in the Middle East today gives some insight into what this was like.) The conflict brought about by the Judaizing teachers over whether Gentiles had to essentially become Jews before becoming Christians was the most obvious and serious issue dealt with in the first century. Acts 15 and the Jerusalem Council describes this clash and how it was solved, but other manifestations of the cultural clash were not absent, including the issues raised in Romans 14-15. Only God could blend so many varied mind-sets from so many cultural heritages into one family, and even he did not do it quickly or easily.

In Romans 15:14, when Paul says, "I myself am convinced, my brothers, that you yourselves are full of goodness, complete in knowledge and competent to instruct one another," his trust in the hearts and motives of his fellow Christians is truly exemplary. No matter what their background, whether Jew or Greek, upright (often uptight!) religious or flagrant pagan, he believed the best of those in Christ. Out of Christ, he was equally candid about these relationships. Titus 3:3 puts it bluntly indeed:

> At one time we too were foolish, disobedient, deceived and enslaved by all kinds of passions and pleasures. We lived in malice and envy, being hated and hating one another.

We have been transformed from haters to lovers, from the hated to the trusted. Is that really how we view one another? Perhaps our early days of serving God was in a youth group, and suspicions may have been developed regarding the commitment of the older group. Perhaps we were in the older group, a bit chaffed and alarmed at the impetuousness of the younger group. Regardless of our attitudes toward people in our pagan days, or in our early religious days, the call is clear: Love and trust one another deeply. Nothing else is the way of Christ.

None of us is exempt from the temptations of prejudice. It may be age prejudice, racial prejudice, educational prejudice, gender prejudice, geographic prejudice or prejudice of some other type. The gospel of Christ calls us to face this sin squarely and just humble out. None of us, regardless of pedigree, is more than an abject sinner if the grace of God applied has not been applied to us. We are not superior in any way to anyone else. The ground is absolutely level at the foot of the cross, where we redeemed sinners beg for mercy. Loving and trusting others is a decision, a decision to practice the *agape* type of love described in 1 Corinthians 13, for this love always trusts. How loving are we? No more loving than we are trusting.

A Constant Sense of Mission (Romans 15:20-33)

²⁰It has always been my ambition to preach the gospel where Christ was not known, so that I would not be building on someone else's foundation. ²¹Rather, as it is written:

"Those who were not told about him will see,
*   and those who have not heard will understand."*

²²This is why I have often been hindered from coming to you.

²³But now that there is no more place for me to work in these regions, and since I have been longing for many years to see you, ²⁴I plan to do so when I go to Spain. I hope to visit you while passing through and to have you assist me on my journey there, after I have enjoyed your company for a while. ²⁵Now, however, I am on my way to Jerusalem in the service of the saints there. ²⁶For Macedonia and Achaia were pleased to make a contribution for the poor among the saints in Jerusalem. ²⁷They were pleased to do it, and indeed they owe it to them. For if the Gentiles have shared in the Jews' spiritual blessings, they owe it to the Jews to share with them their material blessings. ²⁸So after I have completed this task and have made sure that they have received this fruit, I will go to Spain and visit you on the way. ²⁹I know that when I come to you, I will come in the full measure of the blessing of Christ.

³⁰I urge you, brothers, by our Lord Jesus Christ and by the love of the Spirit, to join me in my struggle by praying to God for me. ³¹Pray that I may be rescued from the unbelievers in Judea and that my service in Jerusalem may be acceptable to the saints there, ³²so that by God's will I may come to you with joy and together with you be refreshed. ³³The God of peace be with you all. Amen.

Paul ties in his challenge to both Jews and Gentiles with his mission—past, present and future. He was a missionary on a mission. His heart's desire was to see the Great Commission fulfilled. When he stayed in one location for awhile, it was either for the purpose of training younger leaders to take his place or to spread the message in their region, as was the case of his two-year sojourn in Ephesus (Acts 19:9-10). He was always thinking ahead of spreading the message to those who had not yet heard it. Those of us in nations like America need so much more of this spirit. Most have heard the name Jesus and associate it with religion, but they know next to nothing about the true Jesus of the Bible. Where is the fire burning in our hearts to share the old story with those for whom it is still new?

You have to be impressed with the even-handedness of Paul in addressing both Jew and Gentile. Back in Romans 9-10, he dished out some pretty hard teachings about the history of Jewish rejection of God, but in Romans 11, he was equally challenging to the Gentiles and their tendency to be self-righteous toward Jews. In Romans 15:26-27, he tells about the Gentile disciples' willingness to collect and send money to the poorer saints in Judea, but sums it up by saying that they actually owe it to them for having heard the gospel through them. In physical families, good parents must learn to avoid favoritism, which is often much easier said than done. Spiritual parents must do the same, and we have Paul to imitate on this one. As a rabbi in whom Judaism was deeply ingrained, he nonetheless was given a mission to the Gentiles, and out of this unlikely combination, he was devoid of favoritism. The key to his admirable ability to maintain the balance was a deep love for both types of people. Love dismantles a whole host of faulty attitudes. May God help us to develop this same type of love and thereby destroy all of our prejudices, especially the subtle ones that Satan deceives us into not even seeing.

Paul closes out this section of Romans with his mission plans for the future. Back in chapter 12, he started discussing our gifts and the attitudes toward one another that these *could* produce (on the negative side) and what they *should* produce. It is all about love—and serving our fellow disciples. We have been taught about the depth of love we need to have (Romans 13), the need to refuse to judge those with different backgrounds and opinions (Romans 14), and now in Romans 15, the essentiality of the acceptance and trust of all who are in Christ. Having addressed this ongoing challenge of loving those who differ from us, he talks of his own love for the lost in terms of ambition and mission.

Spiritual ambition is both a divine demand and a tricky trail. Jesus was so ambitious to change the world that it consumed his every waking moment. He never wasted time with the mundane and never wavered from an absolute focus to bring every human being into a confrontation with eternal choices. Paul imitated this in his Lord better than any other human in Scripture, at least in my opinion. Our ambitions, like the apostles in Matthew 20:20-28, are often mixed at best. However, this struggle does not diminish in any way our need for ambition—lots of it. We live in a world with billions of people who do not know God. Every church must have a plan to do something about this horrendous situation, and this means that every ministry group and every disciple in that church must have a carefully formulated plan that is bathed in daily prayer and drenched with the sweat of hard work in carrying it out. A growing love for the lost spells a diminishing selfish ambition.

Pray and share your faith; share your faith and pray. Force yourself far enough out of your comfort zone to necessitate praying continually (1 Thessalonians 5:17). Share your faith enough to ensure not just successes, but failures. Constant rejection does two important things: it makes us appreciate deeply the positive responses to our sharing, and it removes the glory of selfish ambition. In the life truly consumed with preaching, the satisfaction of knowing that we are colaborers with Christ, doing the only thing that matters, is all that remains. We need to pray that God will give us the ambitions of his Son and of his apostle to the Gentiles! Then we will relish the mission on the one hand, while longing for the battle to be over on the other. This was Paul's perspective—desiring to live for the purpose of having fruitful labor and desiring to die to be with his Lord (Philippians 1:20-23). Let all of our ambitions be weighed by these same extremes, and God will be glorified by our efforts.

Romans 15 seems at first glance to be fairly unrelated to what preceded it and what follows it. However, as is always the case with Romans, it is a carefully reasoned treatise designed to explain the nature of faith and the practical application of it.

Romans 12 is about a faith that loves; Romans 13 is about a faith that submits; Romans 14 is about a faith that dismantles disputes over opinion differences; Romans 15 is about a faith that loves in spite of those differences; and Romans 16 is about a faith that delights in relationships. Contextually, it fits together perfectly. When we do "accept one another, then, just as Christ accepted [us]" (Romans 15:7), we can deeply appreciate the ensuing relationships that such acceptance produces. To that topic we now move in the final chapter.

16

Develop and Protect God's Family
Romans 16

Romans 16 seems at first glance to contain little practical material. Paul just mentions a number of people with whom he had relationships in the past. Viewed in this way, the chapter appears to be little more than a farewell ending of an otherwise meaty epistle. The Holy Spirit who inspired Paul knows everything, but he is not focused on trivia. This chapter is pregnant with meaning, providing insights into what it means to be a part of God's family.

The New Testament has many descriptions and designations for what we commonly call "the church," and each has special meaning. Literally the Greek word for church, *ecclesia*, means the "called out." It came to be used to described an "assembly" called out for a unique purpose. The word thus calls attention to both our separateness from the world and our assembling as a group to worship and serve God corporately.

The idea that we are a "kingdom" is developed in passages like Hebrews 12:22-29. This stresses our obedience, as we are the subjects of a King who rules through his law. Too many otherwise religious people have lost their fear and reverence for God and need to be reminded that our King is "a consuming fire" (Hebrews 12:29). But we also need to be reminded that we are both subjects of the King and also his heirs, for he has "raised us up with Christ and seated us with him in the heavenly realms in Christ Jesus" (Ephesians 2:6).

Further, we are the body of Christ, knit together in unity of purpose and love with each other in a way that none is inferior and none is superior (1 Corinthians 12:12-27). Because we are Jesus' spiritual body, we can be serving and saving people all over the globe at the same time, and in this way, doing greater things than he did while he was limited to a physical body (John 14:12).

Then, we are also called "a temple" or "a building of God" (Ephesians 2:19-22). This designation emphasizes our holiness, our righteousness. We are in the world to influence the world, not of the world to be influenced by it.

Agricultural metaphors are also used powerfully. We are "the field" of 1 Corinthians 3:5-15, suggesting hard work and productivity for our Savior (2 Timothy 2:6). Similarly, we are "the vineyard" of Luke 13:6-9 and John 15. Branches tied in to Jesus produce fruit to the glory of God.

One of the most treasured descriptions of the church should be as the bride of Christ (Ephesians 5:25-32, Revelation 19:7). We are married to Jesus, awaiting his coming and the marriage supper of the Lamb.

While all of these definitions of the church are vital, Ephesians 3:14-15 suggests the one that hits my heart the most personally: "For this reason I kneel before the Father, from whom his whole family in heaven and on earth derives its name." I grew up in a dysfunctional family. I knew a brand of love, but not the unconditional love of a perfect Father and not the love of a host of imperfect but devoted siblings. The call of the hour in our movement seems to be that of building family. Examining the numbers of those who have left the Lord has forced this issue at last, when the Bible should have produced it earlier and better than we allowed it to.

A part of our tardiness in figuring this out may trace back to our tendency to view the church in yet another way—as an army, out to spiritually conquer the world. While it is true that we have a commission (a great one at that—Matthew 28:18-20) and must wear the "armor of God" (Ephesians 6:10-17), to put the major emphasis on the church being like an army creates something that can subtly undermine the principles of building a true family. I think that this perspective runs deeper than we might think, making a significant impact on our mode of operation in trying to evangelize the world. A country's military branch actually deemphasizes relationships to ensure the completion of the mission, no matter what the personal cost to any individual or family. But the military is not a Spirit-driven organization and does not exist, as does the church, to specifically help the weak, the sick, the helpless and the lost. Fundamentally, every resource of an army is put toward capturing and conquering the enemy. Every resource of the church is designed to heal and to build. We are about building families that build villages, that impact nations. We need to keep this straight, and Paul in Romans 16 provides just the help that we need.

Servants, One and All (Romans 16:1-16)

16:1I commend to you our sister Phoebe, a servant of the church in Cenchrea. 2I ask you to receive her in the Lord in a way worthy of the saints and to give her any help she may need from you, for she has been a great help to many people, including me.

> *3Greet Priscilla and Aquila, my fellow workers in Christ Jesus. 4They risked their lives for me. Not only I but all the churches of the Gentiles are grateful to them.*
> *5Greet also the church that meets at their house.*
> *Greet my dear friend Epenetus, who was the first convert to Christ in the province of Asia.*
> *6Greet Mary, who worked very hard for you.*
> *7Greet Andronicus and Junias, my relatives who have been in prison with me. They are outstanding among the apostles, and they were in Christ before I was.*
> *8Greet Ampliatus, whom I love in the Lord.*
> *9Greet Urbanus, our fellow worker in Christ, and my dear friend Stachys.*
> *10Greet Apelles, tested and approved in Christ.*
> *Greet those who belong to the household of Aristobulus.*
> *11Greet Herodion, my relative.*
> *Greet those in the household of Narcissus who are in the Lord.*
> *12Greet Tryphena and Tryphosa, those women who work hard in the Lord.*

> *Greet my dear friend Persis, another woman who has*
> *worked very hard in the Lord.*
> [13]*Greet Rufus, chosen in the Lord, and his mother,*
> *who has been a mother to me, too.*
> [14]*Greet Asyncritus, Phlegon, Hermes, Patrobas,*
> *Hermas and the brothers with them.*
> [15]*Greet Philologus, Julia, Nereus and his sister, and*
> *Olympas and all the saints with them.*
> [16]*Greet one another with a holy kiss.*
> *All the churches of Christ send greetings.*

In these brief verses, Paul mentions by name no less than twenty-seven people. Certainly, since he had never been to Rome, he wanted to build as much rapport as possible, and a good way of doing that is to mention those known both by him and by the Roman church. Such networking does pave the way to building a personal relationship more quickly and more deeply. But Paul's mention of these people was not a relational trick of the trade—it was his heart. Above all, he understood relationships—the need for them and the ways to build them. No greater gift can be given than a heart on a platter. No wonder Satan works so hard to make us prideful, insecure and fearful about letting one another in at the deepest emotional level.

Frankly, it is difficult to trust someone who will not let you in, and many are those who verbalize love while remaining emotionally closed to you. And then they wonder why people are not drawn to them! If I do not know who you are, how can I be drawn to you? Read back through Paul's writings, and notice his vulnerability and his unashamed expressions of devotion to people. We have a lot to learn about building family. Eating food together, enjoying a game or movie together, or talking about the Bible or the church together are all good things to do. Families ought to play together and pray together. But mark it down: If you do not get out of your self-imposed protective emotional shell and let others in, family will never be family, and the deepest needs of your soul will go unmet!

As we begin to examine the names in Romans 16, all that we are going to focus on is relationship. Whether Phoebe was an official "deaconness" or simply a good-hearted servant—from the

Greek word meaning "deacon" in its masculine form—is not what is most important (v1). You can trace out the varied itinerary of Aquila and Priscilla on your own, and it is interesting in its own right. What strikes my heart (and I hope, yours) is the deep relationships that just jump off the page.

"Phoebe, a servant of the church in Cenchrea…a great help to many people, including me," writes Paul (vv1-2). Here was a sister who served people, a true leader of women, not by title, but by life. Somehow in the providence of God, she crossed paths with Paul and found her way into his heart. Whatever her sacrifices, she was the loved sister of the greatest man who walked on earth outside Jesus himself (one man's opinion). What a woman she must have been! She had been known in a church prior to Paul's greeting here, but forever after, she was known to the world. Those who humble themselves will be exalted by God, pretty much in direct proportion to the amount of humility exerted, and servant-hood is the acid test of humility.

Next come Priscilla and Aquila, highly esteemed in the NT Hall of Fame (vv3-5). Fellow workers in Christ Jesus, willing to go anywhere, do anything, give up everything—willing to risk their lives for their buddy Paul. Real relationships destroy the clergy/laity mentality. Based on our ongoing, persistent terminology, this couple had not achieved the status of "full-time ministry." However, in the heart of God and of Paul, they were full time, supporting themselves as they moved all over the world to carry out the mission. We need to ask God to help us to do everything possible (including changing our terminology) to reduce and hopefully eliminate any vestige of second-class citizenry in the family of God. Interestingly, of the six mentions of this couple, including Romans 16, Priscilla is mentioned first four times. My guess is that she was the more outspoken of the two, a precedent not without its modern examples!

Next, we are introduced to Epenetus, "the first convert to Christ in the province of Asia" (v5). Acts 19 describes Paul's entry into Asia the first time, on his third mission trip, but we read nothing about Epenetus there. The brother may not have received public recognition earlier, but he kept serving for more spiritual reasons, and then God exalted him to the status of being remembered by millions for thousands of years. Men may not know your name, but "God is not unjust; he will not forget your work and the love you have shown him as you have helped his people and continue to help them" (Hebrews 6:10). I am one of those guys whose name is known, primarily because I am an author. I envy those who serve without recognition for their labors, for I suspect their reward will be greater. Epenetus received recognition, but he did not seek it. Are you *seeking* it?

Mary, mentioned next, is remembered for her hard work (v6). Like Jesus before him, Paul had many women friends, as shown by this very list. I treasure the relationships I have with sisters. By God's grace, I get to be a father figure and a grandfather figure to the younger ones, in fulfillment of Mark 10:29-30. I love women. I love my wife in that unique romantic way that has been honed and polished by thirty-six years of marriage. I fell in love with her forty years ago this fall, but met her first in the third grade—fifty years ago! She is the love of my life. I cannot even think of life without her—I cannot even allow my mind to go there. If it ever has to, I pray it is not for long.

I love our daughter, Renee, who is a bubbly, outspoken, uninhibited wisp of a girl who delights my heart. She is a daddy's girl, to be sure, but a special wife to our son by marriage, one Jeffery Klinkhammer—who is as much a character as she! I love our daughter by marriage, Joy, who is as pure-hearted as her mother, Echie, a disciple in the Guam church, and as Joy's mother by marriage, my wife, Theresa. She is beautiful inside and out, the answer to twenty-five years of prayers for our son, Bryan, to find just the right wife. The two of them have a sensitivity level that I can only long for at this point in my life. And of course, I love my little granddaughter, Aleea, who so looks like her mom did twenty-nine years ago that looking into her eyes goes somewhere deep inside me and stirs something that I think somehow must relate to eternity.

I think of hundreds of sisters in God's family, who like Mary, have worked hard in serving me and mine. As the years go by, I seem to enjoy the company of women almost more than that of men, probably because women do not worry about being macho or strong, as we men foolishly perceive it. They are more unafraid of letting you into their hearts. I think they are naturally purer and more spiritually inclined, and I am drawn to the Jesus in them. Brothers, you and I need to imitate them more and work harder to be the kind of servants women typically are.

In verse 7, Paul introduces us to Andronicus and Junias, his relatives who had been in prison with him, known to be outstanding among the apostles,[1] Christians before he was. Can you imagine being a relative of Paul, fellow jailbird, known by the apostles? What could be better? Only being the child of a king, the King of the universe, the Creator of the ages, who filled the skies so full of stars that man will never find nor even fathom more than a small percentage of them. We know God and are known by God (Galatians 4:9). It no doubt was heartwarming for these two to be known by Paul and the apostles, but God and his Spirit and his Son know you and me. That's not bad, is it? Maybe Andronicus and Junias (some think Junias may have been a woman—if so, perhaps the wife of Andronicus) shared the gospel first with Paul when he was a fire-breathing dragon of a persecutor. Maybe Paul was stirred to a greater hatred of God's movement because his own flesh and blood became Jesus people. Maybe. OGK ("only God knows"). What is not a maybe is their commitment to Jesus Christ and his kingdom.

Next is Ampliatus, known simply as one whom Paul loved in the Lord (v8). That is enough. That is a lot—loved by Paul. Then comes one Urbanus, Paul's fellow worker in Christ (v9). A trusted friend, a fellow soldier, one who was not afraid of getting his hands dirty, willing to serve at his inconvenience in any way needed, whether easy or hard. Yes, I know that the text does not say all of that, but a sold-out fool for Christ (1 Corinthians 4:10) like Paul had little time for those without that kind of commitment and work ethic. Just ask John Mark about that one (Acts 15:36-40).

Stachys was Paul's dear friend (v9); Apelles was tested and approved in Christ, by whatever fiery trials (v10). Aristobulus was blessed to have his household in Christ with him, including perhaps both family and servants (v10). Herodion, like Andronicus and Junias, was a relative of the great apostle (v11). I think of Curt and Janet, and Bill and Donna, in the Dallas church, who proudly introduce themselves as my relatives. I am glad that they are proud of me, for I am very proud of them—relatives whose humility allowed them to be influenced by one whom they knew all too well in his BC days (before Christ), but were graceful enough to look past that unfortunate mess to what God wrought in later years. (Thanks, guys, you light up my life, and so do your kiddos!)

Another man influenced his whole family, someone named Narcissus (v11). That was not an easy name to wear, but he apparently gave it a whole new meaning. Next are Tryphena and Tryphosa, another two women (perhaps twins) who worked hard in the Lord, as the sisters have always done (v12). In some way, they are the weaker vessels, said Peter (1 Peter 3:7 KJV), but in most ways they are the stronger, or so it seems to me. On purely an emotional basis, I would rather be judged as Theresa than as Gordon. Spiritually, my wife is the stronger of the two of us. I think that most of the incredible blessings God has poured out on us trace back to her heart, and to bless her, God is willing to slosh it onto me too.

Paul is on a roll in his recognition of women, as he greets Persis, his dear friend, another woman who worked very hard in the Lord (v12). What can we say? Several men in Paul's list are said to be workers, but all who are specifically said to have *worked hard* are women. This is Paul's emphasis, not mine. The fairer sex outworks us hurly, burly guys, who tend to be more selfish. (Brothers, you know it is true, but I just hope you realize we can change.)

Rufus was chosen in the Lord, blessed with a Christian mother, who had been a mother to Paul as well (v13). Years ago, my two children gave me a ring engraved with the word "Dad." It was symbolic. They knew I was not just a dad to them, but to many. They, like Rufus, are willing to share their parents. Sometimes they call to ask that we spiritually adopt their friends who either have no parents or have parents who do not know Biblically how to love. I applaud our children for understanding this spiritual principle so well and for remaining so unselfish. I am glad that they are raising our grandchildren. I want their hearts in those little ones.

"Asyncritus, Phlegon, Hermes, Patrobas, Hermas and the brothers with them" are mentioned next—all heroes to Paul (v14).

These brothers were known by Paul and the church in Rome, but especially by God. The list of those greeted ends with these: "Philologus, Julia, Nereus and his sister, and Olympas and all the saints with them" (v15). Except for the mention of their names, their lives are unknown to us. In the military cemetery at Normandy, France, where the movie *Saving Private Ryan* begins, many tombstones simply say "Known but to God." If we are disciples known only to God, this is quite enough. Praise God for his family, for those who love and serve, and for those who keep no records of their own good deeds. In Matthew 25:34-40, those who were commended for serving did not remember much about doing it, for it had become second nature to them. They did not simply serve; they became servants. We need to ask God to help us to be such and to build relationships the way Paul did. If I could find a time machine, I would go back and simply carry Paul's luggage from place to place in order to watch him love people. No finer university of learning the real lessons of life could be found than that—unless we found ourselves carrying the luggage of the Master himself!

Final Admonitions (Romans 16:17-27)

> [17]I urge you, brothers, to watch out for those who cause divisions and put obstacles in your way that are contrary to the teaching you have learned. Keep away from them. [18]For such people are not serving our Lord Christ, but their own appetites. By smooth talk and flattery they deceive the minds of naive people. [19]Everyone has heard about your obedience, so I am full of joy over you; but I want you to be wise about what is good, and innocent about what is evil.
> [20]The God of peace will soon crush Satan under your feet.
> The grace of our Lord Jesus be with you.
> [21]Timothy, my fellow worker, sends his greetings to you, as do Lucius, Jason and Sosipater, my relatives.
> [22]I, Tertius, who wrote down this letter, greet you in the Lord.
> [23]Gaius, whose hospitality I and the whole church here enjoy, sends you his greetings.

> *Erastus, who is the city's director of public works, and our brother Quartus send you their greetings.*
> [25]*Now to him who is able to establish you by my gospel and the proclamation of Jesus Christ, according to the revelation of the mystery hidden for long ages past,* [26]*but now revealed and made known through the prophetic writings by the command of the eternal God, so that all nations might believe and obey him—*[27]*to the only wise God be glory forever through Jesus Christ! Amen.*

The relationships mentioned by Paul, representative of relationships in the Roman church, were so precious that no one could be allowed to destroy them (vv17-20). In this passage, Paul does not state that the divisive false teachers are in the fellowship of the church, nor that they are to be excluded from such. Neither does he mention any action to be taken in reaching out to them or warning them. He apparently left this issue somewhat undefined in order to allow the directions in the passage to be applied as needed to anyone causing divisions and putting obstacles in the way of Christians. The passage will fit a member of the church who becomes destructive to the faith of others, a former member who is destructive or even a total outsider. The focus is not specifically on the identity of the sinful person, but rather on the damage he or she is causing, which cannot be neglected. Divisive teaching is smooth and subtle in its genesis, but damaging and damning in its revelation.[2]

Paul closes out his letter by mentioning eight collaborators in his entourage at the time of writing. Add these greeters to the twenty-seven greeted, and you find in one chapter of Romans the names of thirty-five people. What seemed to be a chapter of little consequence is a weighty testimony of what the book of Romans is all about. It shows what happens when we understand the God of all grace and respond to him in loving faith. When he as our Father accepts us as children with the full rights of heirs, we suddenly drop into a family numbering thousands, prepared to give love and receive love in the most unexpected and unique ways imaginable. Oh, sure, we all still have a long way to go in showing the love of Christ to one another and to the world, but the kingdom is by far the best thing I have ever found or have even heard about. Count me in—for time and for eternity.

Love me, and help me to love you. And in the meantime, PBPWM—GINFWMY! ("Please be patient with me—God is not finished with me yet.") God bless you, Paul! I am unworthy to tie your shoes, but I want to imitate you as you imitated our God-man, Jesus the Christ. We are on the road with you and to you, and there is no turning back now.

May we finish our lives as Paul finished this letter, with a focus on evangelism (vv25-27). Like the God of all grace of whom he wrote, this apostle of grace never lost sight of the mission. Seeking and saving the lost is the only possible response of love for the disciple who understands both the damning nature of sin and the loving nature of God. When you get Romans, God will get you. Does he have you? I pray that he now has all who read this book. Praise God for his grace, and may it set all of our hearts free!

Notes

1. The sentence could be taken two ways: one, they were known to be outstanding by the apostles; or two, they could have been known to be outstanding *as* apostles. The word "apostle" means simply "one sent on a mission." Like the word "disciple," "apostle" was used in both a specialized sense (the twelve apostles or the twelve disciples) or in a broader sense. In this broader usage, several outside the Twelve (or thirteen, or fourteen—counting Matthias and Paul) were called apostles. Acts 14:14 includes Barnabas as an apostle, and in 1 Thessalonians 2:6, Paul seemed to include his coworkers as apostles.

2. For a more thorough treatment of the subject of church discipline, see appendix 2.

Appendix 1

Purposes of the Mosaic Law

Positive Purposes of the Law

1. The law provided a basis of fellowship with God through its tabernacle ministry and sacrificial system.
2. It revealed the holy nature of God and called for man to imitate him.
3. It provided a suitable religious nomenclature, which would be needed for those early generations and for those who would receive the New Testament.
4. Future purposes included the use of typology of persons, objects and ordinances.
   - A "type" may properly be defined as a person, institution or event in the old dispensation that was designed to prefigure a corresponding person, institution or event in the new.
   - The book of Hebrews abounds with typology, such as Melchizedek being a type of Christ (Hebrews 5:5-10, 6:20, 7:1-17) and the Most Holy Place of the tabernacle representing heaven (Hebrews 6:19-20, 9:8, 24).
   - The Holy Place in the tabernacle was a type of the church (Acts 15:16-17; 1 Corinthians 3:16; 1 Timothy 3:15).
   - The bronze serpent, lifted up in the wilderness, through which the people found physical healing (Numbers 21:8) was a type of the lifted-up Christ (John 3:14, 12:32).
   - The study of typology is interesting indeed, but beyond the scope of our present study.
5. Prophecies of different kinds paved the way for the Messiah and his NT kingdom.
   - Generally speaking, the word "prophecy" simply denotes one person speaking for another.
   - In Exodus 4:15-16, God described the prophetic process as he told Moses just how he and his brother, Aaron, would work together:

   "You shall speak to him and put words in his mouth; I will help both of you speak and will teach you what to do. He will speak to the people for you, and it will be as if he were your mouth and as if you were God to him."

- Therefore, a prophet was a person who spoke (and/or wrote) the words of God to the people.
- Within straightforward predictive prophecy (as distinguished from typology), several variations can be noted in the Old Testament.
  - ❖ First is the *single* fulfillment style, in which only one specific future event or situation is in view. Most predictive prophecy falls into this category.
  - ❖ Second is the *double* fulfillment style, in which one application is found in the near future, and then another later fulfillment is also intended and applied by God.
    - * See 2 Samuel 7:12-13 for an example of this type—Solomon is immediately in view, but Jesus is the ultimate fulfillment.
    - * Many examples occur when the return from captivity is intertwined with a future messianic view in the background.
      - ⇨ Obviously, the latter is dependent in many ways on the former.
      - ⇨ It is like looking at a snapshot, where the foreground and background are in view in the one picture.
      - ⇨ Great examples of this type prophecy abound: Jeremiah 3:14-18, 16:14-15, 23:7-8; Hosea 1:10-11, 3:4-5; Amos 9:8-15; Micah 5:2-5; Haggai 2:1-9; Zechariah 2:10-12, 6:12-13, 8:1-23.
  - ❖ Third is the *typical* fulfillment style, in which a later situation is a type of earlier Scripture. In this case, the later application would not have been obvious at all had not the man of God thus applied it.
    - * See Matthew 2:15, where Hosea 11:1 is quoted.
      - ⇨ In Hosea, the reference is to Israel leaving Egypt to become a nation, and in Matthew, the reference is to Jesus leaving Egypt as a child and returning to Nazareth.
      - ⇨ In the original setting, we could not have guessed that God would have made the later application as a fulfillment, but he had it in mind all along.
    - * Look now at Deuteronomy 18:15-22, where Joshua is in view as the immediate fulfillment of this passage, but will be followed by a chain of prophets throughout the OT period.
      - ⇨ However, when we come to the New Testament, we find that Jesus was the ultimate fulfillment of Deuteronomy 18 (Acts 3:22-26).
      - ⇨ While we may wonder how anyone could see a future Great Prophet in the passage, the first century Jews clearly did (John 1:21).

    * Next, see Isaiah 7:14, quoted in Matthew 1:22-23.

       ⇨ In the Revised Standard Version of 1952, the Hebrew word *almah* is translated "young woman," which led to a significant controversy among conservative Biblical scholars.

       ⇨ Two issues are at stake: the Hebrew term itself and the context of Isaiah 7.

       ⇨ The term does mean basically "young, unmarried woman of marriageable age," which in that setting presupposed that the person was a virgin.

       ⇨ The context is quite conclusive in showing that this is clearly a typical fulfillment, in that no one would figure out the virgin birth of Jesus was in view in Isaiah.

       ⇨ Essentially, a young, unmarried woman (a virgin) was to marry and have a baby, and before he would be old enough to tell the difference between good and evil, the northern Aram-Israel alliance would be destroyed.

       ⇨ The alliance was broken in 732 BC when Tiglath-Pileser III destroyed Damascus.

       ⇨ Centuries later, the Holy Spirit led Matthew to quote Isaiah 7:14 as a statement that was also true of a birth to a woman who was still a virgin.

       ⇨ Other passages are not in the strict sense a fulfillment of prophecies, but involve similar unexpected applications of OT passages.

       ⇨ Look at Romans 3:10-23—these OT passages in this chain quotation apply to the enemies of God, but here in Romans 3, to everyone.

       ⇨ See also Galatians 3:10-12.

       ⇨ In Leviticus 18:5 and Deuteronomy 27:26, God simply asked the people to be faithfully obedient, not legalistically perfect.

       ⇨ However, in Galatians 3:10-12, the application of these passages is made that when one trusts his works as the basis of his standing with God, then God does in fact demand perfection. (Legalism is a mind-set, and a deadly one at that!)

- Unless we are able to see the difference in the original quotes and the NT application of them, we are going to misunderstand God's use of prophecy in such passages.

6. The law provided examples and thus motivation for NT disciples.

- Warnings and admonitions are found (1 Corinthians 10:1-11; Hebrews 2:1-3, 12:25-29), as are positive lessons (Romans 15:4).

- The number of allusions and citations to OT events, characters and precepts further illustrates this purpose.
7. Additionally, God's civil legislation governed the people with constitutional laws for governmental organization, social laws and criminal laws.
   - The social laws regulated such matters as family life, sexual activity, theft and slavery.
   - The criminal statutes were strongly prohibitive through severe penalties, often requiring the death penalty.
     - ❖ In general; the underlying principle of Mosaic justice appeared to be what is sometimes technically called *justalionis*, the law of compensation.
     - ❖ This provided protection for the weak, and the guilty were guarded against punishment more severe than deserved.
     - ❖ While the OT principle of "an eye for an eye and a tooth for a tooth" may seem severe to us, it was much fairer and actually restrained than many extant laws within pagan societies during the OT historical period.

Negative Purposes of the Law

1. The purposes of the law that were more negative in design related directly to the problem of sin.
   - Law restrained sin, thus keeping the nation separate from other nations around it.
     - ❖ Israel had to be kept distinct to guard God's people from the idolatry that was rampant in virtually all the nations around them.
     - ❖ This separateness also enabled the lineage of Christ to be traceable.
   - The law certainly revealed sin (Romans 7), but it also increased sin in at least two ways: (1) by increasing the statutes and therefore the ways of committing sin and (2) by increasing the desire to rebel in the hearts of those tending to be rebellious. (See Romans 5:20, 7:7-8.)
     - ❖ The express design of the increase was to take captive all things under sin and thus demonstrate the need for a Savior (Galatians 3:22).
     - ❖ Just how much despair was produced in the average Jew, or even in Paul, is a matter of opinion, but if Romans 7 is applied by Paul to his pre-Christian days, then after his conversion the view was made far clearer in retrospect.
     - ❖ Other passages similarly show the present tense being used in referring to past situations to make the point stronger—Matthew

17:11-12, Romans 5:14, 1 Corinthians 13:12, 2 Corinthians 3:7-14, Hebrews 10:9-10.

2. The law had multiple purposes, which were paradoxical at the very least. It could produce despair and delight, frustration and relief, depending on how it was viewed and employed by the individuals under it.

Appendix 2

Love: Disciplined by Limiting Relationships

This material was originally published in my booklet
Love One Another

Here we will consider the topic of church discipline, or as it is often called, "withdrawal of fellowship." This topic is obviously not a pleasant one, but it is a necessary one and a Biblical one. In Protestant churches, the concept of church discipline has often been called the "forgotten commandment." In most churches, including ours, the concept could accurately be called the "misunderstood commandment." Therefore, our task will be to clear up both ignorance about the subject and misconceptions surrounding it. Raising and answering several key questions will hopefully clear up the misunderstandings of this sobering Biblical doctrine.

What Is Church Discipline?

In a broad sense church discipline includes all efforts to train Christians in the way of the Lord, just as the discipline of children includes all training. In the more specific sense that we are considering, it means the purposeful exclusion of a church member from the fellowship of other Christians because of unrepentant sin after Biblical procedures have been followed. To those who have not studied what the Bible has to say on this subject, this definition may sound unloving, judgmental or harsh. However, the Bible rules out any of these responses as being valid.

In Proverbs 13:24, we are told that the one who withholds punishment from his child actually hates the child. The same would be true in the case of spiritual children. Although a type of judging is forbidden by God (Matthew 7:1-2), the judging which would relate to church discipline is clearly demanded by God (1 Corinthians 5:12-13).

As to the charge of harshness, consider some of God's disciplinary actions in the Bible. In the Old Testament, we have the accounts of the flood; Sodom and Gomorrah; Achan (Joshua 7); Korah, Dathan and

Abiram (Numbers 16); and many others like them in which God was very direct and very strong in his response to sin. In the New Testament, God's customary approach is to wait until the Judgment Day before dealing directly and forcefully with sin, but the case of Ananias and Sapphira in Acts 5 should convince us that the nature of God and his hatred of sin has not changed in our day. After looking at such accounts, it becomes obvious that most of us do not see clearly both the "kindness" and the "sternness" of God (Romans 11:22).

Key Biblical Texts
Matthew 18:15–17

If your brother sins against you, go to him privately for the purpose of bringing about reconciliation between the two of you. (The phrase "against you" is not necessarily in the original Greek manuscript.) If he does not repent, take others with you in attempting to resolve the situation. If this approach fails, share the situation with the church. Ultimately, lack of repentance demands that withdrawal of fellowship be practiced.

Romans 16:17–19

In this passage we are taught to watch and to avoid those who cause divisions by their false teachings. Note that Paul does not state that the divisive and false teachers are in the fellowship of the church, nor that they are to be excluded from such. Neither does he mention any action to be taken in reaching out to them or warning them. Therefore, he apparently left this issue somewhat undefined in order to allow the directions in the passage to be applied as needed—to anyone causing divisions and putting obstacles in the way of Christians. The passage will fit a member of the church who becomes destructive to the faith of others, a former member who is destructive or even a total outsider. The focus is not specifically on the identity of the sinful person, but rather on the damage he causes, which cannot be neglected.

1 Corinthians 5:1–13

The sin here is sexual in nature, as a man was sleeping with his father's wife—evidently his step-mother. The church failed to deal responsibly with the sin—they were prideful about the matter (proud of their understanding of grace?). Paul's response was unmistakable:

> But now I am writing you that you must not associate with anyone who calls himself a brother but is sexually immoral or

greedy, an idolater or a slanderer, a drunkard or a swindler.
With such a man do not even eat. (1 Corinthians 5:11)

2 Thessalonians 3:6, 14

In this context Paul addressed a situation in which some people in the church were idle and not even looking for work. The first response to the problem was to refuse to feed such a person—*no work, no food!* (v10). The second response was to take special note of this idle person who refused to obey Paul's instructions and to stop associating with him until and unless he repented. Other passages will be dealt with further here, but these provide us with clear directions about the need for, and nature of, this type of church discipline.

Which Sins Necessitate Withdrawal?

Some sins are mentioned specifically in connection with the withdrawal of fellowship. As we have already seen, both idleness and immorality are grounds for withdrawal, unless repentance occurs.

In 1 Corinthians 5:11, in addition to sexual immorality, other sins are listed, including greed, idolatry, slander, drunkenness and swindling. (In passing, it is interesting to ask how Christians would recognize the sin of greed in another's life. Materialistic attitudes would be a part of the answer, but the level of financial contribution would be involved as well.) In Titus 3:10, a divisive person is to be warned once, then a second time, and if repentance is not produced, then the church is to have nothing to do with him. Romans 16:17-19 is similar, but would be applied to anyone destroying the church, whether a disciple, a former disciple or a nondisciple.

Some sins are not specifically identified with withdrawal, yet are included by necessity because of their impact on a person's relationship with God. Withdrawal of fellowship is actually a recognition that a person has already lost fellowship with God due to unrepentant sin. Therefore, the church cannot be in fellowship with someone who is out of fellowship with God. Many sins would qualify for this category, because most of the sin lists end with admonitions like this: "those who live like this will not inherit the kingdom of God" (see 1 Corinthians 6:9-10, Galatians 5:19-21). Obviously, not all sins are easily observed and some may never be seen by other disciples. But in this case, God will ultimately handle those situations, as 1 Timothy 5:24 states: "The sins of some men are obvious, reaching the place of judgment ahead of them; the sins of others trail behind them." In the sin passages and the discipline passages, it is abundantly clear that known, unrepentant sin cannot be tolerated by the church.

What Is the Procedure for Withdrawal?

When considering administering church discipline, we must first pray for the people (1 John 5:16). Second, we need to go to them and try to turn them back (Matthew 18:15-17, James 5:19-20). We must make sure that we go in a spiritual manner (Galatians 6:1-2). We must also be gentle, careful about our own lives (not self-righteous), and willing to help carry whatever burdens the ones in sin are carrying. Third, we need to take others—leaders—with us as the needs dictate. Fourth, if they are not moved to repentance at this point, we must warn them (1 Thessalonians 5:14, Titus 3:10). Fifth, after they have been warned and have refused to heed the warning, we must inform the church and allow the church to tell us to stay away from those in sin. After they are formally withdrawn from, no social fellowship is allowed (Matthew 18:17; Romans 16:17; 1 Corinthians 5:11; 2 Thessalonians 3:14; Titus 3:10). What is our attitude toward them then? What can we do to help them at this point? We must not regard them as enemies, but we need to continue to pray for them, and when we do see them, we must warn them as fallen brothers (2 Thessalonians 3:15).

What Are the Purposes for Withdrawal?

The reason for the withdrawal of fellowship is for the purpose of obeying God. He commands it. Refusing to obey his teachings on the subject may appear broad-minded and nonjudgmental, but it is unspiritual and rebellious. Our society is so existential that taking almost any stand for Biblical righteousness is labeled as bigotry. Our concern must not be what the world will think of us if we practice church discipline; it must be what God will think of us if we do not!

Next, a purpose for withdrawal is to keep the church pure—in two ways. First, it protects the church from sinful influence (1 Corinthians 5:6). In this passage, sin is compared to yeast, which works through an entire batch of dough. Once unrepentant sin enters the body through one person, Satan gains easier access into other members of the body. There is a spiritual principle involved that is subtle to the casual observer, but devastating in its results during a period of time. When sin is not purged, it leads to a toleration of sin. Toleration leads to an acceptance of sin, and finally, the acceptance leads to the practice of sin! Second, it protects the church from guilt as an accomplice (2 John 9-11).

Another purpose of withdrawal is to serve as a warning to the church (1 Timothy 5:19-20). It is also to show the world that disciples are totally committed to living for God and his mission on the earth. In 1 Corinthians 5:1, Paul was highly upset about their lack of example before the world—they were doing worse things than the world was! In Acts 5:1-10, God practiced some church discipline very directly when he killed Ananias and Sapphira. "Great fear seized the whole church *and all* who heard about these events" (v11, emphasis added). The church was highly regarded by the non-Christians, though they were afraid to join the church for a while! (v13). Nevertheless, the church continued to grow "more and more" (v14).

Finally, the purpose for withdrawal is to restore the fallen Christian if at all possible. Notice the hopeful wording regarding restoration in the following passages: Matthew 18:15; 1 Corinthians 5:5 (see 1 Timothy 1:20 for similar wording); 2 Thessalonians 3:14; and James 5:19. However, this highly desirable result does not happen the majority of the time in real life situations. When this serious act of discipline fails to move the person to repentance, the Bible has not failed; the church has not failed; God has not failed! Only the *person* has failed, by failing to respond to the love of God expressed through the church (Revelation 3:19, "Those whom I love I rebuke and discipline.").

Withdrawal of fellowship is a last resort, much like an emergency operation. The odds are not good for survival, but sometimes it saves a life and therefore must be tried. However, even when repentance and restoration does not occur, all of the other purposes of such discipline are still accomplished and the victory is still the Lord's!

Who Are We?

Discipleship Publications International (DPI) began publishing in 1993. We are a nonprofit Christian publisher affiliated with the International Churches of Christ, committed to publishing and distributing materials that honor God, lift up Jesus Christ and show how his message practically applies to all areas of life. We have a deep conviction that no one changes life like Jesus and that the implementation of his teaching will revolutionize any life, any marriage, any family and any singles household.

Since our beginning, we have published more than 110 titles; plus, we have produced a number of important, spiritual audio products. More than one million volumes have been printed, and our works have been translated into more than a dozen languages—international is not just a part of our name! Our books are shipped regularly to every inhabited continent.

To see a more detailed description of our works, find us on the World Wide Web at www.dpibooks.org. You can order books by calling 1-888-DPI-BOOK twenty-four hours a day. From outside the U.S., call 978-670-8840 ext. 227 during Boston-area business hours.

We appreciate the hundreds of comments we have received from readers. We would love to hear from you. Here are other ways to get in touch:

Mail: DPI, 2 Sterling Road, Billerica, Mass. 01862-2595
E-Mail: dpibooks@icoc.org

Find Us on the
World Wide Web

www.dpibooks.org

1-888-DPI-BOOK

Outside the U.S.,
call 978-670-8840 ext. 227

Faith Saves
conditions exist p 127-128